Bar Exam Comeback

The Retaker's Guide to Finally Passing

Caine Audrey Lehnert

Copyright © 2025 by Caine Audrey Lehnert. All rights reserved.

This book is designed to provide general guidance and strategies for bar examination preparation. The content is based on general principles of test preparation and study methodology. Individual results may vary significantly based on personal circumstances, study habits, aptitude, and numerous other factors beyond the author's control.

The author makes no representations, warranties, or guarantees regarding the effectiveness of the strategies, methods, or advice contained in this book. There is no guarantee that following the guidance in this book will result in passing any bar examination. Bar exam success depends on many factors including but not limited to individual preparation, knowledge base, test-taking ability, and examination-specific conditions.

Bar examinations vary significantly by jurisdiction in terms of format, content, passing requirements, and administration procedures. While this book provides general strategies that may be applicable across different jurisdictions, readers must consult their specific jurisdiction's bar examiners for current, accurate, and official information regarding:

- Examination format and content
- Passing score requirements
- Application procedures and deadlines
- Accommodation request processes
- Retake policies and procedures
- Character and fitness requirements

While the author has made every effort to ensure the accuracy of the information presented, legal education requirements, bar examination procedures, and related policies change frequently. Readers are responsible for verifying current requirements and procedures with appropriate official sources.

The names and scenarios depicted in this book are purely for illustrative purposes only. Any resemblance to actual persons, living or dead, or actual events is purely **coincidental.** All case studies, examples, and success stories presented in this book are fictional composites created for educational purposes. While these examples are based on common patterns and experiences in bar exam preparation, they do not represent actual individuals or specific real-world situations.

Readers acknowledge that they are solely responsible for their bar examination preparation, performance, and results. The decision to follow any strategies or advice contained in this book is made at the reader's own risk and discretion.

Isohan Publishing
ISBN: 978-1-7641437-6-9

Table of Contents

Chapter 1: The Retaker's Reality 1

Chapter 2: What Went Wrong? A Comprehensive Post-Mortem 8

Chapter 3: Rebuilding Confidence After Setback 21

Chapter 4: The Retaker's Study Framework 32

Chapter 5: Targeted Knowledge Building 43

Chapter 6: MBE Strategy Overhaul 56

Chapter 7: Managing Test Anxiety and Mental Performance 71

Chapter 8: Essay Writing Mastery for Retakers 87

Chapter 9: The Final Month - Retaker's Intensive Prep 102

Chapter 10: Test Day Execution 117

Chapter 11: Results and Next Steps 133

Appendix A: Diagnostic Tools and Worksheets 147

Appendix B: Resources for Retakers 165

Appendix C: Success Stories Collection 179

Reference 205

Chapter 1: The Retaker's Reality

You're not broken. You're not stupid. You're not a failure destined to repeat the same mistakes forever. You're a human being who took a test and didn't pass it the first time—and you know what? That happens to thousands of smart, capable people every single exam cycle.

Let me tell you something that might surprise you: approximately 30% of first-time bar exam takers don't pass on their initial attempt (1). That means if you lined up ten people taking the bar for the first time, three of them would be joining you in retaker status. You're in good company, and you're facing a challenge that has absolutely nothing to do with your intelligence or your potential as a lawyer.

The problem isn't you—it's how you've been thinking about this whole situation.

The Numbers Don't Lie (And They Don't Judge)

Bar exam statistics tell a story that most prep companies don't want you to hear because it doesn't sell their "foolproof" methods. The national average first-time pass rate hovers between 68-72%, depending on the jurisdiction and the specific exam administration (2). But here's what gets interesting: retakers who approach their second attempt strategically pass at rates of 60-65% (3).

Think about that for a moment. If you're reading this book, you've already demonstrated that you can get through law school, pass the MPRE, and navigate the complex bar application process. You're not starting from zero—you're starting from a position of knowledge and experience that first-time takers don't have.

California, notorious for its challenging bar exam, sees first-time pass rates that sometimes dip into the 50s (4). New York's February exam consistently shows lower pass rates than July administrations (5). These aren't personal failures—they're statistical realities that reflect the difficulty of the test, not the worth of the test-takers.

Consider Sarah, a law school graduate who scored in the top 25% of her class but failed the bar by three points. She spent weeks convinced she wasn't "smart enough" to be a lawyer. The reality? She took the exam during a particularly difficult administration where the pass rate dropped 8% from the previous year (6). Her "failure" had more to do with timing and test construction than her legal knowledge.

Why Standard Prep Fails Retakers

Most bar prep courses and materials assume you're starting fresh. They're designed for people who need to learn the law from scratch, memorize basic concepts, and develop test-taking skills for the first time. But you're not that person anymore.

You've already sat through hundreds of hours of lectures. You've already made thousands of flashcards. You've already taken dozens of practice tests. The traditional approach of "more of the same" often leads to diminishing returns and, worse, complete burnout.

Standard prep advice tells you to start over completely, as if your previous preparation was worthless. This creates several problems:

The Boredom Problem: You're reviewing material you already know reasonably well, which creates a false sense of security and wastes precious study time on concepts you've already mastered.

The Confidence Problem: When you're reviewing basic concepts you learned months ago, you might think you're doing great because everything seems familiar. But familiarity isn't the same as the ability to apply knowledge under pressure.

The Time Problem: If you're working while studying for your retake (which most people are), you can't afford to spend 400+ hours on material you've already covered. You need targeted, efficient study methods.

Take Michael's example. After failing his first attempt, he enrolled in the same bar prep course again and completed 95% of the assignments. He failed again—by a larger margin. The problem wasn't his effort or dedication; it was that he was using a first-timer's approach as a retaker. He needed targeted practice on his weak areas, not another complete review of subjects he already understood.

Reframing Failure as Data

Here's a radical idea: your bar exam failure wasn't a failure at all. It was an expensive but highly detailed diagnostic test that provided you with specific information about what you need to work on.

Most people view their failed bar exam as evidence of their inadequacy. But what if you viewed it as evidence of exactly what you need to fix? Your score breakdown isn't a judgment on your potential as a lawyer—it's a roadmap for your retake strategy.

When you shift from "I failed because I'm not good enough" to "I failed because I need to improve specific skills," everything changes. Suddenly, you're not dealing with some vague, overwhelming problem. You're dealing with concrete, solvable issues.

Let's look at Jessica's score breakdown:

- MBE: 132 (needed 140)
- Essays: 62% (needed 65%)
- Performance Test: 58% (needed 65%)

Instead of seeing this as "I failed everything," Jessica learned to read it as: "I need 8 more points on MBE, 3 percentage points on essays, and 7 percentage points on performance tests." These became her specific, measurable goals.

The MBE score told her that her substantive knowledge was mostly solid—she wasn't far off. The essay score suggested she understood the law but might have issues with organization or time management. The performance test score indicated she might struggle with reading comprehension under pressure or time allocation.

This data-driven approach transforms your retake from an emotional ordeal into a practical problem-solving exercise.

Setting Realistic Expectations for Your Retake Journey

You need to know what you're signing up for, and it's not what most people think. Your retake journey will probably take 3-6 months of focused study, depending on your score gap and available study time (7). This isn't a quick fix, but it's also not an insurmountable challenge.

Most successful retakers study 15-25 hours per week, which is significantly less than the 40+ hours per week that first-timers often put in (8). The difference is efficiency and focus. You're not learning everything from scratch—you're diagnosing problems and fixing them systematically.

You should also expect some emotional ups and downs. There will be days when you feel confident and motivated, and days when you question everything. This is normal and doesn't predict your ultimate success. The key is developing strategies to manage these fluctuations rather than letting them derail your preparation.

Here's what realistic expectations look like:

- **Study duration**: 3-6 months of focused preparation
- **Weekly time commitment**: 15-25 hours for most people
- **Emotional experience**: Variable, with both confident and doubtful days
- **Progress pattern**: Not linear—you'll have breakthroughs and plateaus
- **Support needs**: More than you might expect—this is not a solo journey

Consider David's timeline. He failed his first attempt in July, took August off to decompress, started targeted studying in September, and passed the February exam. His total study time was about 300 hours spread over four months—far less than his first attempt but much more strategic.

Your retake isn't about proving you're smart enough to be a lawyer. You already proved that by getting through law school. Your retake is about demonstrating that you can identify problems, develop solutions, and execute them effectively. These are exactly the skills that make someone a good lawyer.

The path forward isn't about working harder—it's about working smarter. You have information now that you didn't have before. You have experience that first-time takers lack. You have the opportunity to approach this test strategically rather than hoping your general preparation will be enough.

You're not starting over. You're building on what you already know, fixing what needs fixing, and preparing to succeed on your own terms.

Moving Forward With Purpose

Your first attempt taught you something valuable: the bar exam isn't just a test of legal knowledge. It's a test of test-taking strategy, time management, stress management, and the ability to perform under pressure. Now you know this, and now you can prepare accordingly.

The most successful retakers don't just study harder—they study differently. They use their score breakdown as a diagnostic tool. They focus on their weak areas while maintaining their strengths. They develop test-taking strategies that work for their specific challenges. They build confidence through targeted practice rather than hoping that more hours will somehow lead to success.

You have the legal knowledge. You have the intelligence. You have the determination. What you need now is the right strategy and the right mindset. The chapters that follow will help you develop both.

You're not behind—you're informed. You're not starting over—you're building on what you already know. You're not broken—you're human. And humans can learn, adapt, and succeed when they approach challenges systematically.

Key Takeaways for Moving Forward

- Approximately 30% of first-time takers don't pass, making you part of a large, capable group
- Retakers who approach their second attempt strategically pass at rates of 60-65%
- Your failed exam provided specific diagnostic information about areas needing improvement
- Standard prep advice fails retakers because it assumes you're starting from zero
- Realistic expectations include 3-6 months of study at 15-25 hours per week
- Success comes from working smarter, not harder, using your previous experience as an advantage

Chapter 2: What Went Wrong? A Comprehensive Post-Mortem

You can't fix what you don't understand. Most people who fail the bar exam make the same mistake: they assume they know what went wrong without actually analyzing the evidence. They say things like "I didn't study enough" or "I'm bad at multiple choice" without looking at their actual performance data.

This kind of vague self-diagnosis leads to vague solutions—and vague solutions don't pass bar exams.

The truth is, bar exam failure usually stems from one or more specific, identifiable problems. Once you identify these problems precisely, you can develop targeted solutions. This chapter will help you conduct a thorough analysis of what actually happened during your first attempt, not what you think happened or what you're afraid happened.

The Self-Assessment Framework

Before you can fix anything, you need to understand exactly what broke down during your first attempt. This isn't about self-punishment or dwelling on mistakes—it's about gathering the information you need to succeed next time.

Most people approach this analysis emotionally, focusing on how they felt during the exam or how disappointed they were with the results. But emotions don't provide actionable data. You need to look at your performance systematically and objectively.

Here's your diagnostic questionnaire. Answer each question honestly, even if the answer makes you uncomfortable:

Knowledge Questions:
1. Which subject areas consistently gave you trouble during practice?
2. Did you find yourself guessing on MBE questions because you didn't know the rule?
3. Were you able to identify the legal issues in essay questions?
4. Did you know the elements of the claims/defenses you needed to discuss?
5. Could you spot the relevant facts in performance test materials?

Application Questions:
1. Did you know the law but struggle to apply it to specific fact patterns?
2. Were your essay conclusions inconsistent with your legal analysis?
3. Did you find yourself writing about irrelevant legal concepts?
4. Were you able to distinguish between similar legal rules?
5. Did you struggle with "except" questions on the MBE?

Time Management Questions:
1. Did you finish all sections of the exam?
2. Were you rushing through the final questions/essays?
3. Did you spend too much time on difficult questions?

4. Were you able to complete practice tests within time limits?
5. Did you have time to review your answers?

Test Anxiety Questions:
1. Did your performance in the exam room match your practice performance?
2. Were you able to think clearly during the exam?
3. Did physical symptoms (sweating, racing heart, etc.) interfere with your performance?
4. Were you able to focus on the questions without getting distracted by worry?
5. Did you find yourself second-guessing answers you felt confident about initially?

Essay Writing Questions:
1. Were your essays well-organized with clear issue statements?
2. Did you fully develop your legal analysis?
3. Were you able to connect facts to legal conclusions?
4. Did you address all parts of multi-part questions?
5. Were your essays the appropriate length?

Rachel's answers revealed a clear pattern. She knew the law cold—she could recite elements and rules without hesitation. But she consistently struggled with "except" questions on the MBE and wrote essays that discussed irrelevant legal concepts. Her problem wasn't knowledge; it was application. She needed to work on reading comprehension and fact analysis, not memorizing more rules.

Common Failure Categories

Most bar exam failures fall into predictable patterns. Understanding these patterns helps you identify which category best describes your situation and develop appropriate solutions.

Knowledge Gaps vs. Application Issues

Many people assume that failure means they don't know enough law. Sometimes that's true, but often it's not. You can know every element of every claim and still fail if you can't apply that knowledge effectively.

Knowledge gaps show up as:

- Consistently missing questions in specific subject areas
- Inability to identify legal issues in fact patterns
- Essays that discuss the wrong legal concepts entirely
- Feeling lost when reading questions

Application issues show up as:

- Knowing the law but reaching wrong conclusions
- Essays that identify correct issues but analyze them poorly
- Multiple choice questions where you narrow it down to two answers but consistently choose the wrong one

- Understanding what the question is asking but not being able to connect the facts to the legal rules

Consider Tom's experience. He failed the bar exam despite scoring in the top 10% on his bar prep course's practice tests. His problem wasn't knowledge—he knew the law better than most people who passed. His problem was that he approached every question like a law school exam, writing lengthy discussions of tangential legal concepts instead of focusing on the specific issues raised by the facts.

Tom needed to learn how to read questions more carefully and tailor his responses to what was actually being asked, not demonstrate everything he knew about the general topic.

Time Management Problems

Time management issues are often misunderstood. Most people think time management means working faster, but that's not usually the solution. Real time management means allocating your time strategically based on the point value and difficulty of different sections.

Poor time management shows up as:

- Not finishing the exam
- Spending 45 minutes on a 30-minute essay
- Rushing through the final portion of any section
- Not having time to review obvious mistakes

Strategic time management looks like:

- Allocating time based on point values
- Moving on from difficult questions when appropriate

- Having 5-10 minutes at the end of each section for review
- Spending appropriate time on easy questions to secure those points

Maria failed her first attempt primarily because she spent 50 minutes on the first essay (worth 30% of the written portion) and only had 25 minutes for the final essay (also worth 30%). She wrote a brilliant first essay but completely bombed the final one because she didn't have enough time to address all the issues.

Her solution wasn't to write faster—it was to set strict time limits and stick to them, even if it meant leaving some analysis underdeveloped in early questions.

Test Anxiety and Mental Blocks

Test anxiety is real, and it can destroy your performance even if you know the material cold. But anxiety manifests differently for different people, and the solutions depend on understanding your specific anxiety patterns.

Cognitive anxiety affects your thinking:

- Mind going blank during the exam
- Inability to recall information you know
- Second-guessing correct answers
- Getting overwhelmed by question complexity

Physical anxiety affects your body:

- Rapid heartbeat or sweating
- Nausea or stomach problems

- Tension headaches
- Fatigue or difficulty concentrating

Emotional anxiety affects your mood:

- Panic attacks or intense fear
- Feeling like you're going to fail before you even start
- Crying or emotional overwhelm during the exam
- Difficulty sleeping the night before

Kevin knew the law perfectly and performed well on practice tests at home. But during the actual exam, his anxiety was so severe that he couldn't focus on the questions. He would read the same sentence five times without understanding it. His problem wasn't knowledge or application—it was managing anxiety so he could access the knowledge he already had.

Essay Writing Weaknesses

Essay writing problems often stem from law school habits that don't work on the bar exam. Law school essays reward depth and creativity; bar exam essays reward organization and completeness.

Common essay problems include:

- Poor organization that makes your analysis hard to follow
- Failing to address all parts of multi-part questions
- Writing too much about easy issues and too little about complex ones
- Not connecting facts to legal conclusions

- Forgetting to state your conclusions clearly

Effective bar exam essays:

- Follow a clear, predictable structure
- Address every issue raised by the facts
- Allocate space based on issue complexity and point value
- Make explicit connections between facts and legal rules
- State conclusions clearly and confidently

Lisa wrote beautiful, nuanced essays that showed deep understanding of legal concepts. Her professors loved her writing style. But she failed the bar exam because her essays were organized like academic papers rather than bar exam answers. She buried her conclusions in complex analysis and spent too much time exploring tangential issues.

She needed to learn that bar exam essays are professional documents, not academic ones, and adjust her writing style accordingly.

Multiple Choice Strategy Errors

MBE strategy errors are often subtle but costly. You might know the law perfectly but still miss questions because of how you approach them.

Common MBE mistakes:

- Not reading questions carefully enough
- Focusing on the wrong part of the fact pattern
- Overthinking straightforward questions

- Not using process of elimination effectively
- Changing correct answers to incorrect ones

Effective MBE strategy:

- Reading the question twice before looking at answer choices
- Identifying the specific legal issue being tested
- Using process of elimination to narrow choices
- Trusting your first instinct when you're confident
- Managing time to allow for review

Marcus consistently scored 65-70% on practice MBE questions but only got 58% on the actual exam. His problem wasn't knowledge—it was strategy. He would read questions quickly, jump to conclusions about what was being asked, and miss subtle distinctions in the answer choices.

He needed to slow down his reading and develop a more systematic approach to analyzing questions, not learn more law.

Analyzing Your Score Breakdown

Your score breakdown is a roadmap, but you need to know how to read it. Most people look at their scores and feel bad about them instead of using them as diagnostic tools.

Here's how to analyze your results systematically:

For the MBE:

- A score below 120 suggests significant knowledge gaps that need to be addressed

- A score of 120-135 suggests you know most of the law but have application or strategy issues
- A score above 135 suggests you're very close and likely need minor adjustments rather than major overhauls

For essays:

- Scores significantly below the passing threshold suggest organizational or time management issues
- Scores slightly below the passing threshold suggest you need to fine-tune your analysis or improve your writing efficiency
- Widely varying scores across different essays suggest inconsistent preparation or time management problems

For performance tests:

- Low scores often indicate reading comprehension or time management issues
- The performance test is very teachable—most people can improve significantly with focused practice

Amanda's breakdown showed MBE: 142, Essays: 58%, Performance Test: 52%. This told her that her legal knowledge was solid (strong MBE score) but she had significant issues with written communication and time management. She needed to focus on writing skills and test-taking strategy, not memorizing more law.

Creating Your Personalized Improvement Plan

Once you've identified your specific problems, you can develop targeted solutions. This isn't about studying everything harder—it's about studying the right things in the right way.

If your primary issue is knowledge gaps:

- Focus on your weakest subject areas first
- Use active learning techniques like practice questions rather than passive review
- Create targeted study materials for your problem areas
- Test yourself frequently to ensure retention

If your primary issue is application:

- Practice more questions in your problem areas
- Focus on understanding why wrong answers are wrong
- Work on reading comprehension and fact analysis
- Practice explaining your reasoning out loud

If your primary issue is time management:

- Practice with strict time limits
- Develop question triage skills
- Work on writing more efficiently
- Practice moving on from difficult questions

If your primary issue is test anxiety:

- Consider working with a counselor or coach

- Practice relaxation techniques
- Simulate test conditions during practice
- Develop coping strategies for anxiety symptoms

If your primary issue is essay writing:
- Study model answers to understand structure
- Practice organizing your thoughts before writing
- Work on writing more concisely
- Focus on connecting facts to legal conclusions

Your improvement plan should be specific, measurable, and realistic. Instead of "improve essays," your plan might say "practice organizing essay responses using IRAC format, spending no more than 5 minutes on outlining per essay."

The Bottom Line About Diagnosis

You can't fix what you don't understand, and you can't understand what you don't analyze honestly. Most people fail the bar exam for specific, identifiable reasons that can be addressed with targeted effort.

Your job isn't to become a different person or to study twice as hard. Your job is to identify exactly what went wrong and develop specific strategies to fix those problems. This diagnostic process isn't punishment—it's preparation for success.

Once you know what your real problems are, you can stop wasting time on generic solutions and start working on targeted fixes. The next chapter will help you rebuild the confidence you need to execute your improvement plan effectively.

Key Takeaways for Targeted Improvement

- Conduct an honest analysis using specific questions rather than general assumptions

- Most failures fall into predictable categories: knowledge gaps, application issues, time management, test anxiety, or writing problems

- Your score breakdown provides specific diagnostic information about where to focus your efforts

- Different problems require different solutions—generic "study harder" approaches rarely work

- Create a personalized improvement plan that addresses your specific weaknesses rather than trying to fix everything at once

Chapter 3: Rebuilding Confidence After Setback

The bar exam didn't just test your legal knowledge—it tested your sense of self-worth. And right now, you might be questioning both your intelligence and your future as a lawyer. This isn't unusual, and it isn't permanent, but it is something you need to address directly.

Confidence isn't just a nice-to-have quality for bar exam retakers. It's a necessary component of success. When you don't believe in your ability to pass, you study less effectively, perform worse under pressure, and give up more easily when things get difficult. But when you rebuild genuine confidence based on realistic self-assessment and targeted improvement, you create the conditions for success.

The key word here is "genuine." We're not talking about false optimism or positive thinking. We're talking about confidence based on evidence, preparation, and a realistic understanding of what you can control.

Processing the Emotional Impact of Failure

Let's be honest about what happened. You studied for months, probably sacrificed social activities and personal time, stressed about the exam, took it with high hopes, and then received news that felt like a punch to the gut. That's not a small thing, and pretending it doesn't hurt won't help you move forward.

The emotional impact of bar exam failure is real and significant. You might be experiencing:

- Shame about not passing on the first try

- Anxiety about having to go through the process again
- Anger at yourself, the exam, or the system
- Sadness about delayed career plans
- Fear that you're not cut out to be a lawyer

These feelings are normal, and they're not evidence that you're weak or unsuited for the legal profession. They're evidence that you're human and that this exam mattered to you.

But here's what's crucial: you can't let these emotions drive your decisions about how to move forward. Emotions provide information, but they're not reliable guides for action. Fear might tell you to give up entirely, while anger might tell you to study exactly the same way but harder. Neither approach is likely to lead to success.

Consider Jennifer's experience. After failing her first attempt, she spent three weeks in what she described as "a shame spiral." She avoided friends and family, convinced that everyone was judging her. She started questioning whether she was smart enough to be a lawyer, despite having graduated in the top third of her law school class.

The turning point came when she realized that her emotional reaction was normal but not helpful. She gave herself permission to feel disappointed while also recognizing that her emotions weren't providing accurate information about her capabilities or her chances of future success.

Understanding Imposter Syndrome

Imposter syndrome—the feeling that you're not qualified to be where you are and that others will eventually discover you're a fraud—affects most people who fail the bar exam. It's particularly common among high achievers who aren't used to significant setbacks.

The bar exam failure feeds imposter syndrome because it seems to confirm your worst fears about yourself. You might think:

- "I don't belong in law school"
- "I'm not as smart as my classmates"
- "I've been fooling everyone all along"
- "I don't deserve to be a lawyer"

But here's the reality: imposter syndrome is based on distorted thinking, not accurate self-assessment. You didn't get through law school by accident. You didn't pass the MPRE by luck. You didn't get accepted to law school because admissions committees made a mistake.

The bar exam is one test on one set of days. It doesn't define your intelligence, your potential, or your worth as a person. It certainly doesn't erase three years of law school performance or predict your ability to be an effective lawyer.

Marcus dealt with severe imposter syndrome after his bar exam failure. He had been one of the stronger students in his class, but failing the bar made him question everything. He started wondering if his good grades were just due to grade inflation or if his professors had been too easy on him.

His breakthrough came when he realized that imposter syndrome was making him focus on the wrong questions. Instead of asking "Am I smart enough to be a lawyer?" he started asking "What specific skills do I need to develop to pass this exam?" The first question led to self-doubt and paralysis. The second question led to productive action.

Developing a Growth Mindset Approach

Carol Dweck's research on mindset provides a powerful framework for approaching your bar exam retake (9). People with a **fixed mindset** believe that intelligence and ability are static—you either have what it takes or you don't. People with a **growth mindset** believe that abilities can be developed through effort and learning.

Fixed mindset thinking sounds like:

- "I'm just not good at standardized tests"
- "Some people are natural test-takers and some aren't"
- "I failed because I'm not smart enough"
- "If I was meant to be a lawyer, I would have passed the first time"

Growth mindset thinking sounds like:

- "I haven't developed effective test-taking strategies yet"
- "I can learn to perform better under pressure"
- "I failed because I need to improve specific skills"
- "This setback is information that will help me succeed next time"

The difference isn't just semantic—it's practical. Fixed mindset thinking leads to giving up when things get difficult because struggle seems to prove your inadequacy. Growth mindset thinking leads to persistence because struggle is seen as part of the learning process.

Sarah's first reaction to her bar exam failure was pure fixed mindset: "I'm obviously not cut out for this. Maybe I should just give up and find a different career." But after some reflection, she was able to reframe the situation: "I have skills that need development. I can learn what I need to learn. This is a setback, not a verdict."

This shift in thinking changed everything. Instead of feeling hopeless, she felt motivated. Instead of avoiding studying because it reminded her of her failure, she approached studying as skill development. Instead of dreading the retake, she saw it as an opportunity to prove what she could accomplish when she approached the challenge strategically.

Building Support Systems

Bar exam retakes can be isolating. You might feel embarrassed about your failure and hesitant to talk about your retake plans. You might worry that others are judging you or that asking for help makes you look weak. But isolation makes everything harder, and you don't have to go through this alone.

Effective support systems for bar exam retakers include:

Professional support:

- Bar exam tutors or coaches who specialize in retakers
- Mental health counselors who understand academic pressure

- Career counselors who can help you maintain perspective about your long-term goals

Peer support:

- Study groups with other retakers who understand your situation
- Online communities for bar exam retakers
- Friends from law school who are supportive and encouraging

Family support:

- Family members who understand your timeline and stress levels
- People who can provide practical support like helping with household tasks during intensive study periods
- Loved ones who can remind you of your strengths when you're feeling discouraged

The key is being selective about who you include in your support system. You need people who are encouraging but realistic, supportive but not enabling, and understanding but not overly sympathetic to the point where they reinforce your negative thinking.

David's family kept saying things like "Don't worry about it, the bar exam doesn't really matter anyway" and "You're smart enough that you'll pass easily next time." They meant well, but their comments weren't helpful because they minimized both the challenge he was facing and the work he needed to do to overcome it.

He found much better support from a study group of other retakers who understood the specific challenges he was facing and could provide both emotional support and practical advice about effective study strategies.

Success Story: From Devastation to Determination

Let me tell you about Lisa, whose story illustrates how dramatically things can change between your first attempt and your retake.

Lisa failed her first bar exam by a significant margin—her MBE score was 118 and her written scores were well below the passing threshold. She was devastated. She had graduated from a well-regarded law school with solid grades and had never experienced this kind of academic failure before.

Her first reaction was emotional. She cried for days, avoided contact with her law school friends, and seriously considered abandoning her legal career entirely. She felt like she had wasted three years of law school and let down everyone who had supported her.

But after about two weeks of this, something shifted. She realized that feeling sorry for herself wasn't helping her situation and wasn't going to help her pass the exam. She decided to approach her retake like a project that needed to be managed rather than a personal crisis that needed to be endured.

First, she analyzed her failure systematically. Her low MBE score told her that she had significant knowledge gaps, particularly in Constitutional Law and Evidence. Her essay scores told her that she knew some law but wasn't applying it effectively or organizing her responses well.

Instead of enrolling in the same bar prep course again, she created a targeted study plan:

- She hired a tutor who specialized in MBE improvement
- She joined a small essay writing workshop
- She practiced performance tests twice a week with timed conditions
- She worked with a counselor to develop anxiety management techniques

But the most important change was her mindset. Instead of seeing the retake as proof of her inadequacy, she saw it as an opportunity to demonstrate her ability to learn from setbacks and improve her performance.

She studied for four months, putting in about 20 hours per week of focused, targeted work. This was actually less time than she had spent preparing for her first attempt, but it was much more strategic and effective.

On her second attempt, her MBE score jumped to 147 and her written scores were well above the passing threshold. She didn't just pass—she passed decisively.

More importantly, she felt like the experience had taught her valuable lessons about resilience, problem-solving, and the importance of strategic thinking that would serve her well in her legal career.

The Confidence-Building Process

Rebuilding confidence after a major setback isn't about convincing yourself that you're wonderful. It's about developing genuine confidence based on evidence of your ability to identify problems, develop solutions, and execute them effectively.

Real confidence comes from:

- Understanding exactly what went wrong the first time
- Developing specific, targeted solutions to those problems
- Practicing new skills until they become automatic
- Seeing improvement in your practice performance
- Building competence through deliberate practice

This process takes time, and it's not always linear. You'll have days when you feel great about your progress and days when you doubt yourself. That's normal and doesn't predict your ultimate success.

The key is to focus on the process rather than the outcome. You can't control whether you'll pass the exam (though you can certainly influence it), but you can control how you prepare. When you focus on executing your preparation plan effectively, confidence builds naturally.

Moving Forward With Realistic Optimism

You have good reason to be optimistic about your retake, but your optimism should be based on realistic assessment and strategic preparation, not wishful thinking.

Here's what you have going for you:

- You understand the format and structure of the exam
- You have specific information about your weaknesses

- You know what it feels like to take the exam under pressure
- You're motivated to succeed in a way that first-time takers often aren't
- You can approach your preparation strategically rather than hoping general preparation will be enough

Your confidence shouldn't be based on the idea that you're guaranteed to pass or that the exam will be easy the second time. It should be based on your ability to learn from experience and improve your performance through targeted effort.

You're not the same person who took the exam the first time. You have more information now. You have more experience. You have the opportunity to approach this challenge with wisdom gained from your previous attempt.

That's not a consolation prize—it's a significant advantage.

Closing Thoughts on Resilience

The bar exam tested more than your legal knowledge. It tested your resilience, your ability to bounce back from setbacks, and your commitment to your goals. By choosing to retake the exam, you're demonstrating all of these qualities.

Resilience isn't about never failing. It's about how you respond when you do fail. It's about your ability to learn from mistakes, adapt your approach, and persist in the face of difficulty. These are exactly the qualities that make someone a good lawyer.

Your bar exam failure was a setback, not a verdict. Your retake is an opportunity to demonstrate not just your legal knowledge, but your character, your determination, and your ability to overcome challenges.

You have the knowledge. You have the intelligence. You have the resilience. What you need now is the right strategy and the confidence to execute it. The next section of this book will help you develop both.

Key Takeaways for Confidence Rebuilding

- Emotional reactions to failure are normal but shouldn't drive your preparation decisions
- Imposter syndrome is based on distorted thinking, not accurate self-assessment
- Growth mindset thinking focuses on skill development rather than fixed abilities
- Effective support systems include professional, peer, and family support
- Real confidence comes from evidence of improvement, not positive thinking
- Your retake experience provides advantages that first-time takers don't have

Chapter 4: The Retaker's Study Framework

You've been studying wrong. Not because you're lazy or stupid, but because you've been using a system designed for people who are learning the law for the first time. You're not those people anymore.

First-time bar exam takers need to absorb massive amounts of legal information from scratch. They need to learn basic concepts, understand how different areas of law relate to each other, and develop fundamental test-taking skills. But you already know most of this stuff. What you need is a completely different approach—one that builds on your existing knowledge while targeting your specific weaknesses with laser precision.

The traditional "start from the beginning and review everything" approach doesn't just waste your time—it can actually hurt your performance by creating false confidence and avoiding the hard work of addressing your real problems.

Why Traditional Study Plans Fail Retakers

Most bar prep programs assume you're starting with zero legal knowledge. They're built around the idea that more exposure equals better performance. So they give you hundreds of hours of lectures, thousands of practice questions, and comprehensive outlines covering every possible topic.

This works reasonably well for first-time takers because they need that broad exposure. But for retakers, this approach creates several serious problems:

The Familiarity Trap: When you review material you've already studied, everything looks familiar. Your brain recognizes the concepts and tricks you into thinking you know them better than you actually do. This false sense of mastery leads to overconfidence and under-preparation in areas where you actually need work.

The Boredom Factor: Reviewing material you already understand is mind-numbing. Your attention wanders, you start going through the motions instead of actively learning, and you waste hours on activities that don't improve your performance.

The Avoidance Problem: Comprehensive review programs let you avoid your weak areas by spending time on subjects you already know well. It's much more comfortable to review Constitutional Law concepts you understand than to tackle Evidence problems that confuse you.

The Time Crunch: If you're working while preparing for your retake (which most people are), you simply don't have 400+ hours to spend on comprehensive review. You need targeted, efficient study methods that give you maximum improvement for your time investment.

Consider Mark's experience. After failing his first attempt, he signed up for the same bar prep course again and completed 98% of the assignments. He watched every lecture, did every practice question, and reviewed every outline. He failed again—by a wider margin than his first attempt.

The problem wasn't his work ethic or his intelligence. The problem was that he spent 300+ hours reviewing material he already knew reasonably well while avoiding the specific areas where he needed improvement. His Constitutional

Law knowledge went from solid to excellent, but his Evidence knowledge stayed weak because he never focused on it specifically.

The 70/30 Rule for Strategic Focus

Here's the framework that successful retakers use: spend 70% of your study time on your weakest areas and 30% on maintenance review of your stronger subjects.

This ratio flies in the face of most bar prep advice, which suggests balanced review across all subjects. But balanced review makes no sense for retakers because your knowledge isn't balanced. You probably know some subjects quite well and others poorly. Your study time should reflect these differences.

The 70% - Intensive Weak Area Focus:

- Identify your 2-3 weakest MBE subjects based on your practice performance
- Focus on your most problematic essay areas
- Spend the majority of your study time on these specific deficiencies
- Use active learning techniques: practice questions, flashcards, and application exercises
- Don't move on until you see measurable improvement

The 30% - Maintenance Review:

- Keep your stronger subjects sharp with periodic review

- Do enough practice questions to maintain your skill level
- Review outlines occasionally to prevent knowledge decay
- Don't spend extensive time on subjects you already know well

Sarah's score breakdown showed she was strong in Constitutional Law and Contracts but weak in Evidence and Criminal Procedure. Instead of reviewing all subjects equally, she spent 70% of her time on Evidence and Criminal Procedure practice questions and only 30% on maintenance review of her stronger areas.

This felt uncomfortable at first because she wasn't seeing the easy wins that came from reviewing familiar material. But after six weeks of focused practice, her Evidence and Criminal Procedure scores improved dramatically while her Constitutional Law and Contracts scores stayed strong with minimal maintenance work.

Creating Efficient Study Schedules for Working Professionals

Most retakers are working while studying, which means you need maximum efficiency from limited study time. The key is creating a schedule that fits your real life rather than an idealized version of your life where you have unlimited time and energy.

Time Reality Check: Most successful retakers study 15-25 hours per week for 3-4 months. This is significantly less than first-time takers but requires much more strategic focus. You can't afford to waste time on ineffective study methods.

Energy Management: Study your hardest subjects when your energy is highest. If you're sharpest in the morning, don't waste that time on easy review material. Use your peak energy for your most challenging work.

Consistency Over Intensity: It's better to study 20 hours per week consistently than to alternate between 40-hour weeks and 5-hour weeks. Your brain needs regular practice to build and maintain skills.

Here's a sample weekly schedule for a working professional studying 20 hours per week:

Monday: 3 hours - MBE practice in weak subjects (evening)
Tuesday: 2 hours - Essay practice and review (evening)
Wednesday: 3 hours - MBE practice in weak subjects (evening) **Thursday**: 2 hours - Performance test practice (evening) **Friday**: Off (rest day) **Saturday**: 6 hours - Mixed practice and review (morning/afternoon) **Sunday**: 4 hours - Maintenance review of strong subjects (afternoon)

This schedule prioritizes weak areas during weekday sessions while using weekend time for comprehensive practice and review. The key is consistency—the same times every week so studying becomes automatic rather than a daily decision.

Avoiding Burnout and Study Fatigue

Burnout is a bigger risk for retakers than first-time takers because you're dealing with the emotional weight of previous failure plus the pressure of limited time. You need strategies to maintain motivation and energy throughout your preparation period.

Signs of Burnout:

- Difficulty concentrating during study sessions
- Feeling overwhelmed by the amount of material to cover
- Procrastinating or avoiding study sessions
- Physical symptoms like headaches or sleep problems
- Emotional symptoms like anxiety, irritability, or depression

Burnout Prevention Strategies:

Take Real Breaks: Schedule time off from studying every week. This isn't wasted time—it's necessary for maintaining peak performance. Your brain needs downtime to consolidate learning and prevent fatigue.

Vary Your Study Methods: Don't spend four hours straight doing MBE questions. Mix different types of activities: practice questions, outline review, essay writing, and performance tests. Variety keeps your brain engaged and prevents monotony.

Track Progress, Not Just Time: Focus on improvement metrics rather than hours studied. Seeing your MBE scores improve from 60% to 75% is more motivating than logging 100 study hours.

Maintain Perspective: Remember that this is temporary. Your retake preparation has a definite end date, and the intensity you're experiencing now won't last forever.

Address Physical Needs: Get enough sleep, eat regularly, and exercise. These aren't luxuries—they're necessary for optimal cognitive performance.

Jessica started her retake preparation with intense motivation, studying 35+ hours per week. After six weeks, she was exhausted, her practice scores had plateaued, and she was starting to dread studying. She realized she was burning out and needed to adjust her approach.

She scaled back to 22 hours per week, took Sundays off completely, and started varying her study activities more. Initially, she worried that studying less would hurt her performance. Instead, her practice scores started improving again because she was studying more efficiently and maintaining better focus during her study sessions.

Success Story: The Part-Time Student's Comeback

Let me tell you about David, who managed a successful retake while working full-time and dealing with significant family responsibilities.

David failed his first bar exam while unemployed and able to study full-time. He had put in over 400 hours of preparation using a traditional bar prep course but failed by a substantial margin. His MBE score was 125 and his written scores were well below the passing threshold.

By the time he was ready for his retake, his situation had changed dramatically. He had found a job as a paralegal, his wife was pregnant with their second child, and he had maybe 15-20 hours per week available for studying. He felt like he was at a huge disadvantage compared to his first attempt when he could study all day.

But David's constraints forced him to be strategic in a way he hadn't been the first time. He couldn't afford to waste time on inefficient study methods or comprehensive review of material he already knew.

First, he analyzed his failure systematically. His MBE breakdown showed he was weakest in Evidence, Criminal Law, and Torts. His essay scores indicated he knew the law but wasn't organizing his responses effectively or managing his time well.

Instead of trying to recreate his first-attempt study schedule, he designed a targeted plan:

Weekday evenings (2 hours, 4 nights per week): Focused MBE practice in his three weakest subjects. No lectures, no outline review—just questions, explanations, and targeted learning of rules he didn't know.

Saturday mornings (4 hours): Essay and performance test practice with strict time limits. He would write essays, compare them to model answers, and identify specific areas for improvement.

Sunday afternoons (2 hours): Maintenance review of his stronger MBE subjects and brief outline review of essay topics.

This gave him 18 hours per week of highly focused study time. He tracked his progress weekly, adjusting his focus based on practice performance rather than trying to cover everything equally.

The key to David's success was ruthless prioritization. He didn't try to learn every possible rule or review every possible topic. He focused intensively on his weakest areas while doing just enough maintenance work to prevent his stronger areas from deteriorating.

After 14 weeks of this targeted preparation, David's practice scores had improved dramatically. His MBE practice tests were consistently in the 140s, and his essays were well-organized and complete.

On his retake, David scored 151 on the MBE and passed the written portion decisively. He had studied significantly fewer hours than his first attempt but had been vastly more strategic and efficient.

Most importantly, David felt like he had learned valuable lessons about strategic thinking and resource management that would serve him well in his legal career. He had turned his constraints into advantages by forcing himself to focus on what really mattered.

The Foundation for Success

Your retake preparation should be built on strategic focus, not heroic effort. You don't need to study harder than everyone else—you need to study smarter. You don't need to know more law than first-time takers—you need to apply the law you already know more effectively.

The framework outlined in this chapter—strategic focus on weak areas, efficient time management, and burnout prevention—creates the foundation for everything else you'll do in your preparation. When you get this foundation right, everything else becomes easier.

You have advantages that first-time takers don't have. You know what the exam feels like. You understand the time pressure. You have specific information about your weaknesses. But these advantages only help if you build your preparation around them strategically.

The next chapter will show you how to use targeted knowledge building techniques to turn your identified weak areas into strengths without wasting time on material you already know well.

Moving Forward With Strategic Intent

Your first attempt taught you that general preparation isn't enough. Your retake will succeed because you're approaching it strategically, focusing your limited time and energy on activities that will have the biggest impact on your performance.

This isn't about working harder—it's about working smarter. It's about using your experience and your score breakdown to guide your preparation rather than hoping that more of the same will somehow lead to different results.

You have the information you need. You have the intelligence to succeed. What you need now is the discipline to stay focused on your weak areas even when it's uncomfortable, and the confidence that strategic preparation will pay off on test day.

Key Takeaways for Strategic Study Design

- Traditional study plans fail retakers because they assume you're starting from zero knowledge
- The 70/30 rule focuses most study time on weak areas while maintaining strong subjects
- Efficient schedules for working professionals require 15-25 hours per week of targeted study
- Burnout prevention is critical and requires real breaks, varied study methods, and progress tracking
- Strategic constraints can become advantages when they force focus on high-impact activities

- Success comes from applying existing knowledge more effectively, not learning more law

Chapter 5: Targeted Knowledge Building

You don't need to learn more law. You need to learn the law you already know in a different way—a way that actually sticks under pressure and applies to the specific fact patterns the bar exam throws at you.

Most retakers make the mistake of thinking their problem is insufficient knowledge. They go back to their outlines, re-read their notes, and try to memorize more rules. But here's the truth: if you made it through law school and studied for your first bar attempt, you probably know 80-90% of the law you need to know. Your problem isn't knowledge—it's accessibility and application.

Knowledge that you can't access under pressure is useless. Knowledge that you can't apply to specific fact patterns won't help you pass. Knowledge that dissolves under stress might as well not exist. This chapter will show you how to transform the legal knowledge you already have into the kind of robust, applicable understanding that actually helps you answer questions correctly.

Moving Beyond Passive Outline Reading

Reading outlines feels productive because you're covering a lot of material and everything looks familiar. But passive reading is one of the least effective ways to build the kind of knowledge you need for the bar exam.

Here's what happens when you read outlines: you recognize concepts you've seen before, your brain says "I know this," and you move on to the next topic. But recognition isn't the same as recall, and recall isn't the same as application. The bar exam doesn't ask you to recognize concepts—it asks you to recall rules under pressure and apply them to complex fact patterns.

The Recognition Trap: When you read "The reasonable person standard is objective," your brain recognizes this concept and tells you that you know it. But can you explain what objective means in this context? Can you distinguish it from subjective standards? Can you apply it to a specific fact pattern? Recognition doesn't answer these questions.

The Familiarity Illusion: The more times you read something, the more familiar it becomes, and familiarity feels like knowledge. But familiarity is just your brain recognizing something you've seen before. It doesn't mean you understand it, can recall it under pressure, or can apply it correctly.

The Coverage Fallacy: Reading comprehensive outlines makes you feel like you're covering all your bases. But coverage isn't the same as mastery. It's better to deeply understand 70% of the testable material than to have superficial familiarity with 100% of it.

Consider Rachel's approach to Constitutional Law. She read her outline cover to cover three times and felt confident about her knowledge. But when she took practice tests, she consistently missed questions about the dormant commerce clause—not because she didn't know the concept existed, but because she couldn't apply the multi-part test to specific fact patterns under time pressure.

The outline told her that the dormant commerce clause "limits state regulation of interstate commerce," but it didn't teach her how to analyze whether a particular state law violated this principle. She needed active learning techniques that forced her to practice application, not more passive reading.

Active Recall Techniques for Legal Concepts

Active recall—the practice of retrieving information from memory rather than simply reviewing it—is one of the most effective learning techniques available (10). For legal concepts, this means testing yourself on rules, elements, and applications rather than just reading about them.

Basic Active Recall Methods:

Self-Testing: After reading about a legal concept, close your materials and write down everything you can remember. Don't just list the rule—explain it, give examples, and identify common exceptions or variations.

Explanation Practice: Pretend you're explaining a legal concept to someone who knows nothing about law. If you can't explain it clearly in simple terms, you don't understand it well enough.

Rule Reconstruction: Given a legal principle, try to reconstruct the complete rule from memory, including all elements, exceptions, and variations. For example, don't just recall "battery requires intent"—reconstruct the complete definition including intent, harmful or offensive contact, and lack of consent.

Application Prediction: Before looking at practice questions, read a fact pattern and predict what legal issues are being tested and how they should be analyzed. Then check your prediction against the model answer.

Let's see how this works with a specific example. Instead of reading "Hearsay is an out-of-court statement offered to prove the truth of the matter asserted," try this active approach:

1. **Self-Test**: Write down the definition of hearsay without looking at any materials
2. **Explain**: Describe why the rule exists and what problem it's trying to solve
3. **Apply**: Create your own example of a hearsay statement and a non-hearsay statement
4. **Distinguish**: Explain how hearsay differs from non-hearsay uses of out-of-court statements
5. **Practice**: Find the hearsay issue in a practice Evidence question

This process takes longer than passive reading, but it builds the kind of robust understanding that actually helps you answer questions correctly.

Spaced Repetition Systems for Retention

Your brain forgets information predictably over time unless you review it at specific intervals. Spaced repetition systems use this knowledge to help you review material just before you're likely to forget it, maximizing retention with minimal time investment (11).

How Spaced Repetition Works:

- Review new information within 24 hours of first learning it

- Review again after 3 days, then 7 days, then 14 days, then 30 days
- If you recall the information easily, increase the interval
- If you struggle to recall it, decrease the interval and review more frequently

Legal Application: Instead of cramming all your Evidence rules in one week and then not reviewing them for a month, use spaced repetition to review smaller chunks of information at increasing intervals. This builds long-term retention with less total study time.

Digital Tools: Apps like Anki or Quizlet can automate spaced repetition scheduling, but you can also create a simple manual system using index cards and a filing system.

Michael used spaced repetition for Constitutional Law after consistently missing questions about the levels of scrutiny for equal protection analysis. Instead of re-reading his outline repeatedly, he created a spaced repetition schedule:

- Day 1: Learn the three levels of scrutiny and their applications
- Day 2: Review and test recall
- Day 5: Test recall again (struggled with intermediate scrutiny)
- Day 8: Review intermediate scrutiny specifically, test all three levels
- Day 15: Test recall of all levels (successful)
- Day 30: Final review before exam

This approach took less total time than repeated outline reading but resulted in much better retention and application ability.

Creating Personalized Flashcard Systems

Effective flashcards for bar exam preparation are different from the simple question-and-answer cards you might have used in college. Legal concepts require cards that test understanding, application, and distinctions rather than simple memorization.

Types of Legal Flashcards:

Rule Cards: Front: "What are the elements of negligence?" Back: Complete rule with explanations and common exceptions

Application Cards: Front: Brief fact pattern. Back: Legal analysis and conclusion

Distinction Cards: Front: "How does assault differ from battery?" Back: Clear explanation of similarities and differences

Exception Cards: Front: "When doesn't the hearsay rule apply?" Back: List of exceptions with examples

Policy Cards: Front: "Why does the attorney-client privilege exist?" Back: Policy rationale and how it affects application

Effective Flashcard Design:

- Make cards specific to your weak areas, not comprehensive coverage of all topics
- Include enough context to make the cards meaningful

- Test application and understanding, not just memorization
- Review regularly using spaced repetition principles
- Update cards based on your practice test performance

Lisa created a targeted flashcard system for Evidence after consistently missing hearsay questions. Instead of making cards for every Evidence rule, she focused specifically on hearsay exceptions and their applications:

Card 1: Front: "Excited utterance exception - when does it apply?" Back: "Statement relating to startling event, made while under stress of excitement, sufficient to eliminate reflection. Must be (1) startling event, (2) statement relates to event, (3) made while still under excitement."

Card 2: Front: "Driver says 'Oh no, I was texting!' immediately after car accident. Hearsay exception?" Back: "Yes, excited utterance. Accident is startling event, statement relates to accident, made immediately while still under stress."

This targeted approach helped her master the specific area where she was struggling without wasting time on Evidence concepts she already understood well.

Using Practice Questions Diagnostically

Most people use practice questions to test their knowledge after they think they've learned it. But practice questions are actually more useful as diagnostic tools that tell you what you need to learn and how you need to learn it.

Diagnostic Question Analysis:

Before You Answer: Read the question and identify what legal concepts are being tested. What do you think you need to know to answer correctly?

After You Answer: Whether you got it right or wrong, analyze why. If you got it right, was it because you knew the rule or because you guessed correctly? If you got it wrong, was it because you didn't know the rule, misapplied it, or misread the question?

Pattern Recognition: After 20-30 questions in a subject area, look for patterns in your mistakes. Are you consistently missing questions about specific topics? Are you making the same analytical errors repeatedly?

Targeted Learning: Use your question analysis to identify exactly what you need to study. Don't just note that you missed a Contracts question—identify whether you missed it because you don't know the mailbox rule, because you can't apply the mailbox rule to complex fact patterns, or because you misread the question.

David used this diagnostic approach with Criminal Law MBE questions. After analyzing 50 practice questions, he noticed a clear pattern: he consistently missed questions about accomplice liability, but not because he didn't know the basic rule. He missed them because he couldn't distinguish between different levels of participation in complex fact patterns.

This diagnostic information told him exactly what to study. Instead of reviewing all of Criminal Law, he focused specifically on accomplice liability fact patterns and practiced distinguishing between principals, accessories before the fact, and accessories after the fact in various scenarios.

Success Story: Conquering Constitutional Law Weaknesses

Let me tell you about Amanda, who transformed her weakest subject into one of her strongest using targeted knowledge building techniques.

Amanda's first bar exam results showed a clear pattern: she was strong in most subjects but consistently weak in Constitutional Law. Her MBE breakdown showed she was getting only 45% of Constitutional Law questions correct, compared to 70-75% in other subjects.

Her first instinct was to re-read her Constitutional Law outline and attend extra lectures on Constitutional Law topics. She spent weeks reviewing cases, reading detailed explanations of doctrines, and trying to memorize complex tests and standards.

But when she took practice tests, her Constitutional Law performance hadn't improved. She was still missing the same types of questions, still getting confused by the same concepts, and still feeling uncertain about her answers.

That's when she realized that passive review wasn't working. She needed to actively build her Constitutional Law knowledge using techniques that would make it accessible under pressure.

Step 1: Diagnostic Analysis Amanda analyzed 100 Constitutional Law MBE questions to identify her specific weaknesses. She discovered that she wasn't weak in

Constitutional Law generally—she was weak in specific areas:

- Equal protection analysis (levels of scrutiny)
- First Amendment free speech (content-based vs. content-neutral restrictions)
- Commerce Clause (dormant commerce clause analysis)
- Due process (procedural vs. substantive)

Step 2: Active Learning Instead of reading about these topics, Amanda used active recall techniques:

- She wrote out the complete analysis for each area from memory
- She created her own fact patterns and worked through the analysis
- She explained each concept out loud as if teaching someone else
- She identified the key distinctions that separated correct from incorrect answers

Step 3: Spaced Repetition Amanda created a review schedule that ensured she practiced these weak areas regularly:

- Constitutional Law practice questions every Monday and Thursday
- Weekly review of her targeted concepts
- Monthly comprehensive review to prevent knowledge decay in other areas

Step 4: Application Practice She focused on practice questions that tested application rather than just recognition:

- Timed Constitutional Law question sets twice per week
- Careful analysis of wrong answers to identify patterns
- Creation of personal notes about common traps and distinctions

The Results After 8 weeks of targeted knowledge building, Amanda's Constitutional Law practice scores had improved from 45% to 78%. More importantly, she felt confident about her Constitutional Law knowledge in a way she never had before.

On her retake, Constitutional Law became one of her strongest subjects. She didn't just pass—she performed well above the minimum requirements in an area that had previously been her greatest weakness.

The key to Amanda's success was recognizing that she didn't need to learn more Constitutional Law—she needed to learn it differently. She needed to build knowledge that was accessible under pressure, applicable to specific fact patterns, and robust enough to withstand the stress of exam conditions.

Building Knowledge That Sticks

The knowledge you build during your retake preparation needs to be different from the knowledge you built for law school or your first bar attempt. It needs to be:

Accessible: You can recall it quickly under pressure without extensive prompting **Applicable**: You can use it to analyze specific fact patterns rather than just recognizing general concepts
Robust: It doesn't disappear when you're stressed, tired, or anxious **Efficient**: You can apply it quickly within the time constraints of the exam

Building this kind of knowledge requires active learning techniques that force you to retrieve, apply, and distinguish legal concepts rather than simply reviewing them passively.

This process is more demanding than passive review, but it's also more effective. When you build knowledge actively, it sticks better, applies more easily, and remains accessible even under the pressure of exam conditions.

Moving Forward With Targeted Mastery

You don't need to become a legal scholar to pass the bar exam. You need to develop targeted mastery of the specific concepts and applications that the exam tests. This means focusing your limited time and energy on active learning techniques that build robust, applicable knowledge rather than passive review techniques that create the illusion of learning.

The next chapter will show you how to apply these knowledge-building principles specifically to MBE strategy, transforming your multiple-choice performance through targeted skill development rather than general preparation.

Key Takeaways for Knowledge Building

- Recognition isn't the same as recall, and recall isn't the same as application under pressure

- Active recall techniques build more robust knowledge than passive outline reading
- Spaced repetition maximizes retention while minimizing total study time
- Effective flashcards test understanding and application, not just memorization
- Practice questions should be used diagnostically to identify specific learning needs
- Targeted knowledge building focuses on weak areas rather than comprehensive review of all topics

Chapter 6: MBE Strategy Overhaul

Your MBE performance isn't just about knowing the law—it's about knowing how to take the test. And most retakers are making the same strategic mistakes that cost them points even when they know the correct legal rules.

The MBE isn't a law school exam that rewards deep analysis and creative thinking. It's a standardized test with predictable patterns, common traps, and specific strategies that can dramatically improve your performance. But you have to approach it as a test-taking challenge, not just a legal knowledge challenge.

If your MBE score was below 140 on your first attempt, you probably have both knowledge gaps and strategy problems. If your score was between 140-150, your issue is almost certainly strategic rather than substantive. And if you scored above 150 but still failed overall, you need to maintain your MBE strength while focusing on written components.

This chapter will show you how to analyze MBE questions systematically, manage your time effectively, and avoid the common traps that catch even well-prepared test-takers.

Common MBE Mistakes Retakers Make

Most retakers approach the MBE the same way they approached it the first time, hoping that more knowledge will somehow lead to better performance. But strategic mistakes often matter more than knowledge gaps, and these mistakes are completely fixable once you recognize them.

Mistake #1: Reading Too Quickly You've seen MBE questions before, so you think you can read them faster than first-time takers. But MBE questions are carefully constructed to include subtle distinctions and specific facts that change the analysis. Speed-reading causes you to miss these crucial details.

Example: A question might ask about a defendant's liability for battery, but the facts show that the plaintiff consented to the contact. If you read quickly and focus on the battery elements, you'll miss the consent issue entirely.

Mistake #2: Overthinking Straightforward Questions Your legal education taught you to spot complex issues and consider multiple perspectives. But many MBE questions are testing basic rule application, not sophisticated legal analysis. Overthinking leads you to create problems that don't exist.

Example: A simple negligence question asks whether a driver who hits a pedestrian while texting is liable. The answer is straightforward—texting while driving is negligent behavior. But some test-takers will start analyzing comparative negligence, assumption of risk, and other complex issues that aren't relevant to the specific question being asked.

Mistake #3: Focusing on the Wrong Facts MBE questions include lots of facts, but only some of them are legally relevant. Retakers often get distracted by interesting but irrelevant details instead of focusing on the facts that actually matter for the legal analysis.

Example: A Contracts question might include detailed information about the parties' personal relationship, but the legal issue turns on whether their agreement satisfies the statute of frauds. Getting caught up in the relationship dynamics causes you to miss the real issue.

Mistake #4: Changing Correct Answers Research shows that your first instinct is usually correct when you're confident about your initial choice (12). But anxiety and overthinking cause many retakers to change correct answers to incorrect ones during review time.

Mistake #5: Poor Answer Choice Analysis Many retakers don't use systematic methods for evaluating answer choices. They read through all four options and go with whichever one "feels right" instead of using elimination techniques and logical analysis.

Question Analysis Techniques

Effective MBE performance requires a systematic approach to reading and analyzing questions. This isn't about speed—it's about accuracy and consistency.

The Two-Read Method:

First Read: Read the question stem (the part that asks the actual question) before reading the fact pattern. This tells you what legal issue to focus on and what facts will be most important.

Second Read: Read the fact pattern carefully, focusing on facts that relate to the legal issue identified in the question stem. Don't get distracted by irrelevant details.

The IRAC Approach for MBE Questions:

Issue: What legal concept is being tested? **Rule:** What rule of law applies to this situation?
Application: How does the rule apply to these specific facts? **Conclusion:** Which answer choice best reflects the correct application?

Systematic Answer Choice Evaluation:

Don't just read through the answer choices looking for one that seems right. Use a systematic approach:

1. **Eliminate Obviously Wrong Choices**: Start by crossing out choices that are clearly incorrect
2. **Identify the Legal Distinction**: Figure out what legal principle distinguishes the remaining choices
3. **Apply Facts to Law**: Determine which choice correctly applies the relevant law to the given facts
4. **Double-Check**: Make sure your chosen answer actually answers the question being asked

Let's see how this works with a sample approach:

Question stem: "Is the defendant liable for battery?"

Analysis: This question is testing battery law. I need to focus on facts related to intent, harmful/offensive contact, and lack of consent.

Fact pattern reading: I'll pay special attention to what the defendant intended, what contact occurred, and whether there was consent.

Answer evaluation: I'll eliminate choices that discuss irrelevant legal concepts, then focus on the choices that correctly apply battery law to these facts.

Time Management Strategies During the Exam

MBE time management isn't about working faster—it's about allocating your time strategically based on question difficulty and your personal strengths and weaknesses.

The Basic Math:

- 200 questions in 6 hours = 1.8 minutes per question average
- But you shouldn't spend the same amount of time on every question
- Easy questions might take 45 seconds; difficult questions might take 3-4 minutes
- You need time at the end for review and any questions you skipped

Time Allocation Strategy:

First Pass (4.5-5 hours): Answer every question you can answer confidently. Skip questions that will require extensive analysis or that you find confusing. Mark skipped questions clearly.

Second Pass (45-60 minutes): Return to skipped questions with fresh eyes. Often, questions that seemed impossible during your first pass will seem manageable after you've warmed up with easier questions.

Final Review (15-30 minutes): Review questions where you changed your answer or weren't completely confident. Don't change answers unless you're certain you made an error.

Question Triage: Learn to recognize different types of questions quickly:

Gimme Questions: You know the answer immediately. Spend 45-60 seconds, choose your answer, and move on.

Standard Questions: You know the relevant law and can work through the analysis systematically. Spend 2-3 minutes, work through your process, and choose your answer.

Time Sinks: Questions that would require extensive analysis or that test obscure legal principles. Skip these initially and return to them if you have time.

Confusion Questions: Questions where you don't understand what's being asked or don't know the relevant law. Skip these and return to them later—sometimes they'll make more sense after you've warmed up.

Educated Guessing Methods

Even with excellent preparation, you'll encounter some questions where you don't know the answer with certainty. Effective guessing strategies can help you pick up additional points on these questions.

Elimination Guessing: If you can eliminate two answer choices as clearly wrong, you have a 50% chance of guessing correctly between the remaining two. This is much better than random guessing (25% chance).

Extreme Answer Elimination: MBE questions usually test mainstream legal principles. Answer choices that use extreme language ("never," "always," "under no circumstances") are often incorrect because legal rules typically have exceptions.

Common Sense Check: If an answer choice would lead to an absurd or grossly unfair result, it's probably wrong. The law generally tries to reach reasonable outcomes, even when applying technical rules.

Consistent Theory Guessing: If you're unsure between two answers, choose the one that's more consistent with the general principles of that area of law. For example, in Constitutional Law, choices that protect individual rights are often correct when you're unsure.

Pattern Recognition: After taking many practice tests, you'll start to notice patterns in how questions are constructed and how correct answers are typically phrased. Trust these patterns when you're guessing.

What NOT to do when guessing:

- Don't spend more than 2-3 minutes trying to figure out a question you don't understand
- Don't change answers during review unless you're certain you made an error
- Don't look for complex exceptions when a straightforward rule application would work
- Don't overthink questions that seem too easy

Practice Question Quality vs. Quantity Approach

Most retakers think they need to do thousands of practice questions to improve their MBE performance. But question quality matters much more than quantity, especially when your study time is limited.

High-Quality Practice Characteristics:

- Questions that match the current MBE format and difficulty level
- Detailed explanations that help you understand why wrong answers are wrong
- Questions that test the most frequently examined concepts

- Practice tests that simulate actual exam conditions

Low-Quality Practice Characteristics:

- Outdated questions that don't reflect current MBE patterns
- Questions that are much easier or harder than actual MBE questions
- Explanations that just restate the rule without explaining the analysis
- Random questions that don't help you identify patterns or weaknesses

The Focused Practice Method: Instead of doing hundreds of random questions, focus your practice strategically:

Diagnostic Phase (Weeks 1-2): Take 2-3 full practice tests to identify your weakest subject areas and question types.

Targeted Practice Phase (Weeks 3-8): Focus most of your question practice on your 2-3 weakest areas. Do 25-50 questions per week in these areas with careful review of explanations.

Integration Phase (Weeks 9-12): Take full practice tests under timed conditions to integrate your improvements and maintain your strong areas.

Review and Analysis: After every practice session, analyze your performance:

- Which types of questions are you missing consistently?
- Are you making knowledge errors or strategy errors?

- Are there patterns in your wrong answers?
- Are you improving in your targeted weak areas?

Success Story: From 120 to 150+ MBE Score

Let me tell you about Kevin, who transformed his MBE performance through strategic analysis and targeted practice.

Kevin's first bar exam MBE score was 122—well below the passing threshold in most jurisdictions. He was devastated because he had studied extensively and felt like he knew the law reasonably well. His initial reaction was to assume he needed to learn more legal rules and memorize more exceptions.

But when Kevin analyzed his practice test performance more carefully, he realized that his problem wasn't primarily knowledge-based. He was getting about 70% of the questions correct in his strong subjects (Constitutional Law and Contracts) but only 45% correct in his weak subjects (Evidence and Criminal Procedure).

More importantly, he noticed patterns in his mistakes that had nothing to do with legal knowledge:

- He was consistently misreading question stems and answering the wrong question
- He was overthinking straightforward questions and creating issues that didn't exist
- He was getting distracted by irrelevant facts instead of focusing on legally significant information
- He was changing correct answers to incorrect ones during review time

Kevin's Strategic Overhaul:

Week 1-2: Diagnostic Analysis Kevin took three full practice MBE tests and analyzed every wrong answer to identify patterns. He discovered that he was making three main types of errors:

1. Misreading questions (25% of wrong answers)
2. Knowledge gaps in Evidence and Criminal Procedure (45% of wrong answers)
3. Strategic errors like overthinking and poor time management (30% of wrong answers)

Week 3-6: Targeted Knowledge Building Instead of reviewing all subjects equally, Kevin focused 70% of his study time on Evidence and Criminal Procedure. He used active learning techniques:

- Created flashcards for Evidence hearsay exceptions and Criminal Procedure constitutional issues
- Practiced explaining complex rules out loud
- Did targeted question sets in these subjects with careful analysis of explanations

Week 7-10: Strategy Development Kevin developed systematic approaches to reading and analyzing questions:

- Always read the question stem first to identify the legal issue
- Underline key facts related to that issue
- Use elimination techniques before selecting an answer

- Set strict time limits and stick to them

Week 11-14: Integration and Practice Kevin took full practice tests under timed conditions, focusing on implementing his new strategies consistently. He tracked his scores by subject and question type to ensure continued improvement.

The Results: Kevin's practice test scores improved steadily:

- Week 2: 122 (baseline)
- Week 6: 135 (after targeted knowledge building)
- Week 10: 148 (after strategy development)
- Week 14: 152 (after integration practice)

On his retake, Kevin scored 156 on the MBE—a 34-point improvement that made the difference between failing and passing decisively.

The key to Kevin's success was recognizing that MBE improvement requires both knowledge building and strategy development. He didn't just study harder—he studied smarter, focusing on his specific weaknesses and developing systematic approaches to test-taking that improved his performance even when he wasn't completely certain about the law.

Developing Consistent Test-Taking Habits

MBE success requires developing habits that become automatic under pressure. When you're stressed and running short on time, you need systematic approaches that you can execute without having to think about them.

Pre-Question Routine:

1. Read question stem first
2. Identify the legal concept being tested
3. Read fact pattern focusing on relevant facts
4. Predict the legal analysis before looking at answers

Answer Evaluation Routine:

1. Read all four answer choices
2. Eliminate obviously wrong choices
3. Identify what distinguishes the remaining choices
4. Choose the answer that best applies the law to the facts

Time Management Routine:

1. Check your pace every 25 questions
2. Skip questions that will take too long initially
3. Return to skipped questions with remaining time
4. Leave 15-20 minutes for final review

Review Routine:

1. Check that you've answered every question
2. Review questions where you changed your answer
3. Trust your first instinct unless you're certain you made an error

These routines need to become so automatic that you don't have to think about them during the exam. Practice them consistently during your preparation so they feel natural under pressure.

Building MBE Confidence

MBE confidence comes from consistent performance, not from hoping you'll get lucky. When you develop systematic approaches to reading questions, analyzing answer choices, and managing your time, your performance becomes more predictable and reliable.

Confidence Builders:

- Consistent improvement in practice test scores
- Systematic approaches that work regardless of question difficulty
- Understanding why you're getting questions right, not just getting them right
- Ability to eliminate wrong answers even when you're not sure about the correct one

Confidence Killers:

- Inconsistent practice performance
- Relying on intuition rather than systematic analysis
- Changing correct answers during review
- Focusing on obscure exceptions rather than mainstream rules

Your goal isn't to get every question right—it's to perform consistently at a level that contributes to overall bar exam success. For most people, this means scoring in the 140s or 150s, which requires getting about 70-75% of questions correct.

This is absolutely achievable with strategic preparation that focuses on your weak areas while maintaining your strengths through systematic test-taking approaches.

The Path to MBE Success

Your MBE improvement will come from two sources: targeted knowledge building in your weak areas and strategic test-taking skill development. Both are necessary, but strategy development often produces faster and more dramatic improvements.

You don't need to become a legal expert to score well on the MBE. You need to become skilled at analyzing MBE questions, identifying the legal issues being tested, and applying mainstream legal principles to specific fact patterns under time pressure.

This is a learnable skill set that improves with focused practice and systematic analysis. When you approach the MBE as a test-taking challenge rather than just a legal knowledge challenge, your performance will improve dramatically.

The next chapter will address the psychological aspects of test performance—managing anxiety, building confidence, and maintaining peak mental performance under pressure.

Key Takeaways for MBE Strategy

- MBE performance depends on both legal knowledge and test-taking strategy
- Common mistakes include reading too quickly, overthinking, and poor answer choice analysis

- Systematic question analysis methods improve accuracy and consistency
- Time management requires strategic allocation based on question difficulty
- Educated guessing techniques can help you gain points on uncertain questions
- Quality of practice questions matters more than quantity
- Consistent improvement comes from targeted practice in weak areas combined with strategic skill development

Chapter 7: Managing Test Anxiety and Mental Performance

Your anxiety isn't a character flaw—it's a normal response to a high-stakes situation that you've already experienced as stressful. But anxiety becomes a problem when it interferes with your ability to demonstrate what you actually know. And for retakers, anxiety often carries extra baggage: the fear of failing again, the pressure of limited opportunities, and the weight of everyone's expectations.

Here's the truth about test anxiety: it's completely manageable with the right techniques, but you have to address it directly rather than hoping it will just go away. Most people try to reduce anxiety by studying more, but knowledge alone doesn't solve anxiety problems. You need specific strategies for managing your mental and physical responses to stress.

The good news is that retakers often have an advantage in managing anxiety because you know what to expect. You've been through this before, you understand the format and timing, and you can prepare specifically for the situations that triggered anxiety during your first attempt.

Identifying Anxiety Triggers Specific to Retakers

Retaker anxiety is different from first-timer anxiety because it's layered with additional fears and expectations. Understanding your specific triggers helps you develop targeted strategies for managing them.

Common Retaker Anxiety Triggers:

Fear of Repeated Failure: The thought "What if I fail again?" can create a cycle of anxiety that interferes with both studying and test performance. This fear often becomes self-fulfilling because anxiety itself impairs performance.

Time Pressure Awareness: Unlike first-timers who might not fully grasp the time constraints, you know exactly how challenging the timing can be. This awareness can create anticipatory anxiety that starts weeks before the exam.

Comparison to Others: You might feel like you're "behind" compared to classmates who passed on their first attempt. This comparison creates shame and self-doubt that fuels anxiety.

External Pressure: Family, friends, and potential employers might be watching your second attempt more closely, creating additional pressure to succeed.

Financial Stakes: The cost of retaking (exam fees, lost work time, delayed career start) can create financial anxiety that compounds test anxiety.

Perfectionism: Some retakers develop perfectionist tendencies, feeling like they need to score much higher this time to "prove" themselves. This perfectionism creates unrealistic expectations and increased anxiety.

Consider Maria's experience. During her first bar exam, she had some nervousness but felt reasonably confident. But as her retake approached, she found herself waking up at 3 AM with racing thoughts about failing again. She started having panic attacks during practice tests—something that never happened during her first preparation.

Maria's anxiety wasn't about the material (she knew the law better than ever) or the format (she understood the exam structure). Her anxiety was specifically about the stakes of retaking and the fear that she might not be capable of passing.

Understanding Your Specific Anxiety Pattern

Not everyone experiences anxiety the same way. Some people have physical symptoms, others have cognitive symptoms, and many have both. Understanding your specific pattern helps you choose the most effective management techniques.

Physical Anxiety Symptoms:

- Rapid heartbeat or palpitations
- Sweating or hot flashes
- Nausea or stomach problems
- Muscle tension or headaches
- Difficulty breathing or feeling short of breath
- Trembling or shaking
- Fatigue or difficulty sleeping

Cognitive Anxiety Symptoms:

- Racing thoughts or mind going blank
- Difficulty concentrating or focusing
- Negative self-talk or catastrophic thinking
- Memory problems or feeling confused
- Indecisiveness or second-guessing

- Intrusive thoughts about failure

Behavioral Anxiety Symptoms:

- Procrastination or avoidance
- Fidgeting or restlessness
- Changes in eating or sleeping patterns
- Social withdrawal or isolation
- Increased irritability or mood swings

Take a moment to identify which symptoms you experienced during your first bar exam and which ones you're experiencing now during preparation. This information will help you choose the most effective anxiety management techniques.

Cognitive Behavioral Techniques for Test Day

Cognitive Behavioral Therapy (CBT) techniques are among the most effective methods for managing test anxiety because they address both the thoughts and behaviors that fuel anxiety (13). You can learn and practice these techniques on your own.

Thought Challenging Techniques:

Identify Catastrophic Thinking: Notice when you're imagining the worst possible outcomes. Thoughts like "If I fail again, my career is over" or "Everyone will think I'm stupid" are examples of catastrophic thinking.

Reality Testing: Ask yourself: Is this thought realistic? What evidence do I have for and against this belief? What would I tell a friend who had this thought?

Perspective Taking: Consider alternative explanations. Instead of "I'm not smart enough to pass," try "I need to adjust my study strategy" or "I'm learning to perform better under pressure."

Present Moment Focus: Anxiety often involves worrying about future events that may never happen. Practice bringing your attention back to what you can control right now.

Practical Application:

Original anxious thought: "I'm going to fail again and everyone will know I'm not cut out for this."

Challenged thought: "I have more knowledge and better strategies than my first attempt. Even if I don't pass this time, it doesn't define my worth or my potential. Many successful lawyers needed multiple attempts."

Behavioral Techniques:

Graded Exposure: Gradually expose yourself to anxiety-provoking situations in controlled ways. Start with short practice tests, then work up to full-length exams under timed conditions.

Relaxation Response: Practice specific relaxation techniques until they become automatic. This might include progressive muscle relaxation, deep breathing, or visualization.

Mindfulness Practice: Learn to observe your thoughts and feelings without getting caught up in them. Mindfulness helps you respond to anxiety rather than react to it.

Physical Preparation and Stress Management

Your body's response to stress can significantly impact your cognitive performance. Physical preparation for test anxiety involves both regular stress management practices and specific techniques for test day.

Daily Stress Management:

Regular Exercise: Physical activity is one of the most effective ways to reduce baseline anxiety levels. Even 20-30 minutes of walking daily can make a significant difference (14).

Sleep Hygiene: Anxiety and sleep problems often feed each other. Establish regular sleep schedules, avoid caffeine late in the day, and create a calming bedtime routine.

Nutrition: Stable blood sugar levels help maintain stable mood and concentration. Avoid excessive caffeine, eat regular meals, and stay hydrated.

Relaxation Practice: Daily relaxation practice (even 10-15 minutes) builds your ability to calm yourself quickly when anxiety arises.

Test Day Physical Techniques:

Box Breathing: Breathe in for 4 counts, hold for 4 counts, breathe out for 4 counts, hold for 4 counts. Repeat 4-6 times. This activates your parasympathetic nervous system and reduces anxiety quickly.

Progressive Muscle Relaxation: Tense and release different muscle groups systematically. Start with your toes and work up to your head, tensing each group for 5 seconds then releasing.

Grounding Techniques: Use your five senses to connect with the present moment. Name 5 things you can see, 4 things you can hear, 3 things you can touch, 2 things you can smell, and 1 thing you can taste.

Movement Breaks: If the exam allows, use bathroom breaks for brief movement and stretching. Even 30 seconds of movement can help reset your nervous system.

Accommodation Options for Anxiety Disorders

If your test anxiety is severe enough to significantly impair your performance, you may be eligible for testing accommodations. These accommodations are designed to level the playing field, not provide an unfair advantage.

Common Accommodations for Anxiety:

- Extended time (typically 50% additional time)
- Separate testing room
- Additional break time
- Permission to bring anxiety medications
- Use of stress-relief items (stress ball, fidget tools)
- Allowing frequent bathroom breaks

Documentation Requirements: Most bar examiners require documentation from a licensed mental health professional that includes:

- Diagnosis of an anxiety disorder
- Description of how the condition impacts test performance
- Specific accommodation recommendations

- History of previous accommodations (if any)

The Application Process:

- Apply for accommodations well in advance (often 3-6 months before the exam)
- Provide complete documentation as requested
- Be prepared to provide additional information if requested
- Understand that accommodation requests are evaluated individually

Important Considerations: Accommodations aren't automatic, and not everyone with test anxiety will qualify. The key is demonstrating that your anxiety significantly impairs your ability to demonstrate your knowledge under standard testing conditions.

Some people worry that using accommodations will affect their bar admission or future employment. In most jurisdictions, accommodation use is confidential and not reported to bar examiners or employers.

If you think you might benefit from accommodations, consult with a mental health professional who has experience with testing accommodations to discuss your options.

Visualization and Mental Rehearsal Techniques

Mental rehearsal allows you to practice successful test performance in your mind, building confidence and reducing anxiety about unknown situations. This technique is used by athletes, performers, and other professionals who need to perform under pressure (15).

Effective Visualization Components:

Vivid Detail: Include sensory details in your visualization. What does the testing room look like? What sounds do you hear? How does your chair feel?

Positive Outcomes: Visualize yourself performing well, staying calm, and successfully completing the exam. See yourself reading questions clearly, applying the law correctly, and managing your time effectively.

Problem-Solving: Include potential challenges in your visualization and see yourself handling them calmly. What if you encounter a difficult question? What if you start feeling anxious during the exam?

Emotional States: Include the emotions you want to experience—confidence, calmness, focus, determination. Feel these emotions during your visualization practice.

Complete Experience: Visualize the entire test day experience from arrival to completion. Include traveling to the test site, checking in, taking breaks, and finishing successfully.

Sample Visualization Script:

"I arrive at the testing center feeling prepared and confident. I check in efficiently and find my assigned seat. The room is comfortable and well-lit. I arrange my materials and take a few deep breaths.

When the exam begins, I read the first question carefully and clearly understand what's being asked. I apply the relevant legal rules to the facts and select my answer confidently. I work through questions systematically, staying focused and calm.

When I encounter a difficult question, I stay calm and use my elimination strategies. I don't panic or rush—I work through my approach methodically. I manage my time well and finish each section with a few minutes to review.

During breaks, I stay relaxed and positive. I use my breathing techniques to maintain calm energy. I feel proud of my preparation and confident in my ability to demonstrate what I know.

At the end of the day, I feel satisfied with my performance. I know I did my best and applied my knowledge effectively."

Mental Rehearsal Practice:

- Practice visualization daily during your preparation period
- Use the same script consistently to build familiarity
- Practice both during relaxed states and when you're slightly stressed
- Include visualization practice before each practice test
- Adapt the script based on your specific concerns or challenges

Success Story: Overcoming Crippling Test Anxiety

Let me tell you about James, whose story shows how severe test anxiety can be overcome with systematic preparation and the right techniques.

James's first bar exam was a disaster—not because he didn't know the law, but because his anxiety was so severe that he couldn't function effectively. He had panic attacks during both the MBE and essay portions, his mind went completely blank during several questions, and he left the exam feeling like he had failed catastrophically.

His scores confirmed his fears: he was significantly below the passing threshold in all areas. But when James analyzed his practice test performance leading up to the exam, he realized something important: his practice scores at home were actually quite good. His problem wasn't knowledge—it was his ability to access that knowledge under the specific stress of the actual exam.

James's anxiety had several specific triggers:

- Fear of time running out (he had always been a slow test-taker)
- Worry about failing again and disappointing his family
- Physical symptoms (rapid heartbeat, sweating) that made it hard to concentrate
- Catastrophic thinking about his career prospects if he failed

James's Systematic Approach to Anxiety Management:

Step 1: Professional Support James worked with a psychologist who specialized in performance anxiety. Together, they identified his specific anxiety patterns and developed a customized treatment plan.

Step 2: Cognitive Restructuring James learned to identify and challenge his catastrophic thoughts. Instead of "If I fail again, my life is ruined," he practiced thinking "This is one test on one day. It doesn't define my worth or my future."

Step 3: Physical Anxiety Management James practiced relaxation techniques daily until they became automatic:

- Box breathing for immediate anxiety relief
- Progressive muscle relaxation for general stress reduction
- Regular exercise to manage baseline anxiety levels

Step 4: Gradual Exposure James gradually exposed himself to test-like conditions:

- Started with untimed practice questions
- Progressed to timed sections
- Eventually took full practice tests under strict time limits
- Practiced in different locations to reduce environmental anxiety

Step 5: Mental Rehearsal James spent 10-15 minutes daily visualizing successful test performance. He included potential challenges in his visualization and practiced staying calm and focused.

Step 6: Test Day Strategy James developed specific strategies for managing anxiety during the actual exam:

- Arrived early to reduce time pressure stress
- Used breathing techniques between sections
- Had a plan for handling panic symptoms if they arose
- Practiced positive self-talk throughout the day

The Results: James's second attempt was completely different from his first. He still felt nervous, but his anxiety was manageable rather than overwhelming. He was able to think clearly, access his knowledge effectively, and complete all sections of the exam.

Most importantly, James felt like himself during the exam. Instead of being controlled by anxiety, he was able to focus on demonstrating what he knew.

James passed his second attempt decisively, scoring well above the minimum requirements. But even more significant was his newfound confidence in his ability to manage anxiety and perform under pressure—skills that served him well throughout his legal career.

Building Mental Resilience for Test Day

Test anxiety management isn't just about reducing negative feelings—it's about building positive mental states that support peak performance. Mental resilience helps you bounce back quickly from challenges during the exam.

Components of Mental Resilience:

Acceptance: Accept that some anxiety is normal and doesn't mean you're unprepared. Fighting anxiety often makes it worse; accepting it often reduces its power.

Flexibility: Have multiple strategies for handling different situations. If one approach isn't working, you can switch to another without panic.

Present-Moment Awareness: Stay focused on the current question rather than worrying about previous questions or future sections.

Self-Compassion: Treat yourself with the same kindness you would show a good friend. Harsh self-criticism increases anxiety and impairs performance.

Realistic Confidence: Build confidence based on your preparation and abilities, not on unrealistic expectations of perfection.

Creating Your Personal Anxiety Management Plan

Your anxiety management plan should be as personalized as your study plan. Different techniques work better for different people, so experiment during your preparation to find what works best for you.

Your plan should include:

Daily practices for managing baseline anxiety levels
Specific techniques for handling anxiety during practice tests
Test day strategies for managing anxiety in the actual exam
Emergency techniques for handling panic or overwhelming anxiety **Support systems** for encouragement and perspective

Plan Development Process:

1. Identify your specific anxiety triggers and symptoms
2. Experiment with different techniques during practice
3. Choose 3-4 techniques that work best for you
4. Practice these techniques until they become automatic
5. Create a written plan for test day implementation

Your anxiety doesn't have to control your performance. With the right preparation and techniques, you can manage anxiety effectively and demonstrate what you actually know on test day.

The Mental Game

Managing test anxiety is as much a skill as legal analysis or time management. Like any skill, it improves with practice and systematic development. You don't need to eliminate anxiety completely—you need to manage it effectively so it doesn't interfere with your performance.

The techniques in this section aren't just for the bar exam. They're life skills that will help you manage stress and perform effectively in challenging situations throughout your legal career. Learning to manage performance anxiety is an investment in your long-term professional success.

The next section will address essay writing mastery—the skills you need to transform your legal knowledge into clear, organized, and persuasive written analysis under time pressure.

Strategic Insights for Mental Performance

- Test anxiety is manageable with specific techniques, not just more studying
- Retakers face unique anxiety triggers related to fear of repeated failure and external pressure
- Cognitive behavioral techniques address both the thoughts and behaviors that fuel anxiety
- Physical preparation includes both daily stress management and test day techniques

- Testing accommodations are available for those with documented anxiety disorders
- Visualization and mental rehearsal build confidence and reduce anxiety about unknown situations
- Mental resilience involves acceptance, flexibility, and present-moment awareness rather than trying to eliminate all anxiety

Chapter 8: Essay Writing Mastery for Retakers

Your essay writing problems aren't about your legal knowledge—they're about translating that knowledge into organized, persuasive analysis under severe time pressure. Most retakers know the law well enough to pass the essays, but they struggle with structure, time management, and the specific writing style that bar examiners expect.

Bar exam essays aren't academic papers that reward creativity and nuanced analysis. They're professional exercises that reward organization, completeness, and efficient application of legal rules to specific facts. Once you understand this distinction and develop the right approach, your essay scores will improve dramatically.

The good news is that essay writing is highly teachable. Unlike the MBE, which requires extensive knowledge across multiple subjects, essay success depends primarily on following a systematic approach that you can learn and practice until it becomes automatic.

Common Essay Pitfalls and How to Avoid Them

Most essay failures stem from predictable mistakes that have nothing to do with legal knowledge. Understanding these pitfalls helps you avoid them and focus your preparation on what actually matters.

Pitfall #1: Law School Essay Habits

Law school essays rewarded depth, creativity, and sophisticated analysis. You could write beautifully crafted discussions that explored multiple perspectives and complex policy considerations. Bar exam essays reward clarity, organization, and complete issue coverage.

Law School Approach: "The contract formation issue presents several interesting considerations. While classical contract theory would suggest..."

Bar Exam Approach: "Contract formation requires offer, acceptance, and consideration. Here, Smith's email constituted an offer because..."

The bar exam wants direct application of legal rules to specific facts, not philosophical discussions about legal theory.

Pitfall #2: Poor Time Management

Many retakers spend too much time on early essays and run out of time for later ones. This happens because they write as if they have unlimited time rather than adjusting their writing style for the time constraints.

Poor Time Management: Spending 50 minutes on a 30-minute essay to write a "perfect" answer **Good Time Management**: Spending exactly 30 minutes and covering all issues adequately

Pitfall #3: Inadequate Issue Identification

Some essays test multiple legal issues, and you need to address all of them to get full credit. Missing issues costs points even if you analyze the issues you do identify perfectly.

How to Avoid: Read fact patterns twice—once to understand the story, once to identify all legal issues. Make a brief outline before writing to ensure you address everything.

Pitfall #4: Poor Organization

Disorganized essays are hard to follow and make it difficult for graders to give you credit for correct analysis. Clear organization makes your analysis easy to follow and demonstrates your understanding.

Poor Organization: Mixing different legal issues together, jumping between topics, or burying conclusions in the middle of analysis **Good Organization**: Addressing each issue separately with clear IRAC structure

Pitfall #5: Insufficient Factual Analysis

Many people state legal rules correctly but fail to connect those rules to the specific facts in meaningful ways. Bar exam essays require explicit connections between law and facts.

Insufficient: "The defendant may be liable for negligence." **Sufficient**: "The defendant may be liable for negligence because his decision to text while driving breached the reasonable standard of care."

Understanding What Bar Examiners Want

Bar examiners aren't looking for brilliant legal insights or creative arguments. They're looking for evidence that you can:

- Identify legal issues quickly and accurately
- State relevant legal rules correctly
- Apply those rules to specific facts systematically
- Reach reasonable conclusions based on your analysis

- Organize your response clearly and efficiently

The Bar Examiner's Perspective: Bar examiners read hundreds of essays and have limited time to grade each one. They need to see your analysis quickly and clearly. Essays that make them work to understand your reasoning get lower scores, even if the reasoning is ultimately correct.

What Gets Rewarded:

- Clear issue identification
- Accurate statement of legal rules
- Explicit application of law to facts
- Logical organization
- Complete coverage of all issues
- Appropriate length and depth for time allocated

What Gets Penalized:

- Missing major legal issues
- Incorrect statements of law
- Failure to apply law to facts
- Poor organization that makes analysis hard to follow
- Spending too much time on minor issues while missing major ones

IRAC Refinement for Clearer Analysis

IRAC (Issue, Rule, Application, Conclusion) isn't just a writing format—it's a thinking tool that helps you analyze legal problems systematically. But many people use IRAC mechanically without understanding how to make it work effectively.

Effective Issue Identification:

Your issue statement should be specific enough to guide your analysis but broad enough to encompass the legal question being asked.

Too Broad: "This raises contract issues." **Too Narrow**: "Did Smith's email on Tuesday constitute a valid offer under the mailbox rule as applied to electronic communications?" **Just Right**: "Did Smith's email constitute a valid offer?"

Strategic Rule Statement:

State the rule in a way that sets up your factual analysis. Include the elements or factors you'll need to discuss, but don't recite every possible exception or variation.

Too Minimal: "A contract requires offer, acceptance, and consideration." **Too Extensive**: "A contract requires offer, acceptance, and consideration. An offer is a manifestation of willingness to enter into a bargain, so made as to justify another person in understanding that his assent to that bargain is invited and will conclude it. The offer must be communicated to the offeree and must be sufficiently definite and certain. Various factors determine..." **Just Right**: "A valid offer requires manifestation of willingness to contract, communication to the offeree, and sufficient definiteness of terms."

Focused Application Section:

This is where most essays succeed or fail. Your application must connect specific facts to specific legal requirements and explain why those connections lead to particular conclusions.

Weak Application: "Smith's email was probably an offer because it showed he wanted to make a contract." **Strong Application**: "Smith's email constituted an offer because it manifested his willingness to be bound ('I will sell'), was communicated directly to Jones, and contained sufficiently definite terms (specific car, specific price, specific timeframe for response)."

Clear Conclusion:

Your conclusion should directly answer the question posed in your issue statement. Don't hedge unnecessarily or provide alternative conclusions unless the facts truly support multiple reasonable outcomes.

Weak Conclusion: "Smith's email might be considered an offer depending on various factors." **Strong Conclusion**: "Smith's email constituted a valid offer."

Time Allocation Strategies for Essay Sections

Effective time management on essay questions requires treating time as a finite resource that must be allocated strategically based on point values and issue complexity.

Basic Time Allocation Framework:

30-minute essays: 5 minutes planning, 20 minutes writing, 5 minutes review **45-minute essays**: 7 minutes planning, 33 minutes writing, 5 minutes review
60-minute essays: 10 minutes planning, 45 minutes writing, 5 minutes review

Planning Time Use:

- Read the question twice (2-3 minutes)
- Identify all legal issues (2-3 minutes)
- Create brief outline showing issue order and approximate space allocation (1-2 minutes)

Writing Time Use:

- Spend time proportional to point values of different issues
- If an essay has three issues worth equal points, spend equal time on each
- Don't spend 15 minutes on a minor issue while giving 5 minutes to a major one

Review Time Use:

- Check that you addressed all issues in your outline
- Look for obvious errors or omissions
- Don't rewrite substantial portions—focus on quick fixes

The Discipline of Time Limits:

Successful essay writers develop the discipline to stop writing when time is up, even if they haven't said everything they wanted to say. An adequate treatment of all issues scores better than a perfect treatment of some issues and no treatment of others.

Practice this discipline during your preparation:

- Set timers for practice essays and stop when time expires

- Practice writing under time pressure rather than taking as long as you need
- Learn to recognize when you have enough analysis rather than trying to be comprehensive

Practice Scheduling and Feedback Incorporation

Essay improvement requires systematic practice with high-quality feedback. Most people don't practice essays enough, and when they do practice, they don't use the feedback effectively.

Effective Essay Practice Schedule:

Week 1-2: Write one essay per week, focus on organization and time management **Week 3-6**: Write two essays per week, focus on issue identification and rule application **Week 7-10**: Write three essays per week, focus on efficiency and completeness **Week 11-12**: Write one full essay exam (3-4 essays) per week under timed conditions

Types of Practice:

Untimed Practice: Initially, focus on learning the structure and approach without time pressure **Timed Practice**: Once you understand the approach, always practice under time constraints **Issue-Spotting Practice**: Practice identifying issues without writing full essays **Rule Recitation Practice**: Practice stating legal rules quickly and accurately

Feedback Sources:

Model Answers: Compare your essays to high-scoring model answers, focusing on organization and issue coverage **Tutors or Courses**: Get personalized feedback on your specific weaknesses **Study Groups**: Exchange essays with other retakers for mutual feedback **Self-Evaluation**: Develop criteria for evaluating your own essays objectively

Using Feedback Effectively:

Focus on Patterns: Look for consistent weaknesses across multiple essays rather than treating each essay as a separate problem **Prioritize Issues**: Work on your biggest problems first (usually organization or time management) before fine-tuning smaller issues **Practice Specific Skills**: If you struggle with issue identification, practice that skill specifically rather than just writing more full essays **Track Improvement**: Keep notes on your progress so you can see improvement over time

Success Story: From Failing Essays to Top Scores

Let me tell you about Patricia, who transformed her essay performance through systematic analysis and targeted practice.

Patricia's first bar exam essay scores were catastrophically low—she failed the written portion by a significant margin despite having solid MBE scores. She was confused because she knew the law well and had been a strong writer in law school.

When Patricia analyzed her failed essays, she discovered several specific problems:

- She was missing major legal issues while spending excessive time on minor ones
- Her organization was confusing, with legal analysis scattered throughout her responses

- She was writing in an academic style that was inefficient for timed conditions
- She consistently ran out of time and left essays incomplete

Patricia's Essay Transformation Process:

Step 1: Diagnostic Analysis Patricia obtained copies of her original essays and compared them to model answers. She made a list of specific problems:

- Missed 40% of major legal issues
- Spent too much time on factual background and not enough on legal analysis
- Used unclear organization that made her analysis hard to follow
- Failed to state legal rules clearly before applying them

Step 2: Model Answer Study Instead of immediately practicing more essays, Patricia studied 20-30 model answers to understand the expected style and approach. She noticed:

- Model answers used clear, direct language rather than academic prose
- Each issue was addressed separately with obvious transitions
- Rule statements were concise but complete
- Factual application was explicit and detailed

Step 3: Systematic Practice Patricia practiced essays systematically, focusing on one skill at a time:

Weeks 1-2: Issue identification practice. She read fact patterns and listed all legal issues without writing full essays.

Weeks 3-4: Organization practice. She wrote detailed outlines for essays but didn't write full responses.

Weeks 5-8: Timed writing practice. She wrote complete essays under time constraints, focusing on clear organization and complete issue coverage.

Weeks 9-12: Integration practice. She wrote full essay exams under actual test conditions.

Step 4: Feedback Integration After each practice essay, Patricia:

- Compared her response to model answers
- Identified specific areas for improvement
- Practiced those specific skills before writing the next essay
- Tracked her progress on key metrics (issues identified, organization clarity, time management)

The Results: Patricia's improvement was dramatic and measurable:

- Issue identification improved from 60% to 95% of major issues spotted
- Organization became clear and easy to follow
- Time management improved—she finished all essays with time for review

- Writing style became concise and effective for timed conditions

On her retake, Patricia's essay scores were not just passing—they were among the highest in her jurisdiction. She had transformed her biggest weakness into a significant strength.

Key Elements of Patricia's Success:

Systematic Diagnosis: She identified specific problems rather than assuming she needed to "write better generally" **Targeted Practice**: She focused on her weakest skills rather than practicing everything equally **Model Answer Study**: She learned the expected style and approach rather than relying on law school writing habits **Consistent Feedback**: She evaluated every practice essay against specific criteria and adjusted her approach accordingly

Developing Your Essay Writing System

Successful essay writing under time pressure requires a systematic approach that you can execute consistently regardless of the specific question content.

Pre-Writing System:

1. Read the question call twice to understand what's being asked
2. Read the fact pattern once for the story, once for legal issues
3. Create a brief outline showing issues and approximate time allocation
4. Set internal deadlines for each section

Writing System:
1. Address each issue separately with clear transitions
2. Use consistent IRAC structure for each issue
3. State rules clearly before applying them
4. Make explicit connections between facts and legal conclusions
5. Keep conclusions direct and definitive

Review System:
1. Check that you addressed all issues from your outline
2. Look for obvious errors or omissions
3. Ensure your handwriting is legible (if handwritten)
4. Don't rewrite large sections—focus on quick fixes

Time Management System:
1. Start with easier issues to build confidence and momentum
2. Allocate time based on point values, not personal interest
3. Set firm deadlines and stick to them
4. Leave some time for review even if you haven't said everything you wanted

This systematic approach reduces the cognitive load of essay writing because you don't have to make decisions about structure or approach during the exam. You can focus your mental energy on legal analysis rather than wondering how to organize your response.

Moving Forward With Essay Confidence

Essay writing success comes from understanding that bar exam essays are a specific type of professional writing that follows predictable patterns. Once you learn these patterns and practice applying them under time pressure, your performance will improve consistently.

You don't need to become a brilliant legal writer to succeed on bar exam essays. You need to become skilled at organizing legal analysis clearly, applying law to facts explicitly, and managing your time effectively. These are learnable skills that improve with focused practice.

The next section will address the final month of preparation—how to taper your study intensity, manage pre-exam anxiety, and optimize your performance during the crucial weeks leading up to your retake.

Strategic Insights for Essay Excellence

- Essay success depends more on organization and time management than legal brilliance
- Bar exam essays reward clear, direct analysis rather than academic writing style
- IRAC structure should guide both thinking and writing for systematic analysis
- Time allocation must be proportional to point values, not personal interest in issues
- Systematic practice with quality feedback produces measurable improvement
- Developing a consistent writing system reduces cognitive load during the exam

- Model answer study teaches expected style and approach more effectively than general writing advice

Chapter 9: The Final Month - Retaker's Intensive Prep

The final month before your retake is not the time for major changes or dramatic new study strategies. It's the time for fine-tuning, confidence building, and mental preparation. Most people make the mistake of either panicking and trying to learn new material or becoming complacent and reducing their efforts too much.

Your goal during this final month is to peak at exactly the right time—feeling confident, sharp, and ready without being burned out or anxious. This requires a careful balance of maintaining your knowledge, practicing under realistic conditions, and managing your mental state.

The retaker's final month is different from a first-timer's because you have the advantage of experience but also the additional pressure of knowing this opportunity matters even more. You need strategies that account for both your knowledge base and your psychological state.

Understanding the Psychology of Final Month Preparation

The final month creates unique psychological pressures that can either help or hurt your performance, depending on how you manage them.

Common Final Month Mental Traps:

The Panic Study Trap: Feeling like you don't know enough and trying to cram new information. This usually backfires because cramming interferes with consolidation of knowledge you already have.

The Overconfidence Trap: Feeling like you know everything and reducing your study intensity too much. This leads to knowledge decay and poor test-taking sharpness.

The Perfectionist Trap: Trying to learn every possible rule and exception instead of focusing on high-yield review. This creates anxiety and takes time away from practice.

The Comparison Trap: Worrying about what other people are doing instead of focusing on your own preparation. This creates unnecessary anxiety and distraction.

Effective Final Month Mindset:

Maintenance and Sharpening: Your goal is to maintain the knowledge you've built while sharpening your test-taking skills and building confidence.

Quality Over Quantity: Focus on high-quality practice and review rather than trying to cover as much material as possible.

Present-Moment Focus: Concentrate on today's preparation rather than worrying about next week or next month.

Process Trust: Trust the preparation process you've been following rather than second-guessing everything in the final weeks.

Tapering Study Intensity Effectively

Tapering means gradually reducing your study intensity as the exam approaches to avoid burnout while maintaining peak performance. This is similar to how athletes taper their training before major competitions.

The Tapering Schedule:

4 Weeks Before: 100% intensity - This is your peak study period. You should be putting in full effort with practice tests, targeted review, and skill refinement.

3 Weeks Before: 85% intensity - Begin slight reduction in study hours while maintaining focus on weak areas. Start incorporating more full-length practice tests.

2 Weeks Before: 70% intensity - Further reduce total study time but increase the proportion spent on test-taking practice rather than learning new material.

1 Week Before: 50% intensity - Light review and confidence-building activities. Focus on mental preparation and maintaining skills rather than improving them.

3 Days Before: 25% intensity - Very light review only. Focus primarily on rest, relaxation, and mental preparation.

Day Before: 10% intensity - Brief, confidence-building review only. Focus on rest and mental preparation.

Sample Tapering Plan:

Month 4 (Peak Intensity - 25 hours/week):

- Monday: 4 hours MBE practice (weak subjects)
- Tuesday: 3 hours essay practice
- Wednesday: 4 hours MBE practice (weak subjects)
- Thursday: 3 hours performance test practice
- Friday: Rest day
- Saturday: 6 hours mixed practice and review

- Sunday: 5 hours maintenance review

Month 3 (Begin Taper - 20 hours/week):

- Monday: 3 hours MBE practice
- Tuesday: 3 hours essay practice
- Wednesday: 3 hours MBE practice
- Thursday: 2 hours performance test practice
- Friday: Rest day
- Saturday: 5 hours full practice test
- Sunday: 4 hours light review

Final Week (Maintenance - 12 hours/week):

- Monday: 2 hours light MBE practice
- Tuesday: 2 hours essay review
- Wednesday: 2 hours light practice
- Thursday: 2 hours confidence-building review
- Friday: 2 hours very light review
- Saturday: 2 hours relaxation and mental preparation
- Sunday: Rest day

The key principle is that your study hours decrease, but the quality and focus of your study time should remain high. Don't use tapering as an excuse to stop working entirely—use it as an opportunity to practice under realistic conditions while avoiding burnout.

Final Review Strategies That Work

Final month review should focus on maintaining and consolidating knowledge rather than learning new material. Your review strategy should be targeted, efficient, and confidence-building.

High-Yield Review Activities:

Flashcard Review: If you've been using flashcards for weak areas, continue reviewing them using spaced repetition. Don't create new flashcards—focus on mastering the ones you already have.

Practice Question Review: Go back through practice questions you missed earlier in your preparation. Can you answer them correctly now? This builds confidence and reinforces learning.

Outline Skimming: Quick review of your main outlines or study materials, focusing on areas where you've had recent difficulties. Don't try to memorize—just refresh your memory.

Pattern Recognition: Review your notes about common question patterns, typical wrong answer choices, and strategic approaches to different question types.

What NOT to Do During Final Review:

Don't Learn New Topics: If you don't know a topic by now, trying to learn it in the final month will likely create confusion and anxiety rather than useful knowledge.

Don't Take Too Many Practice Tests: One or two full practice tests during the final month is sufficient. More than that can create fatigue and anxiety without providing useful information.

Don't Obsess Over Weak Areas: Continue working on weak areas, but don't let anxiety about them dominate your preparation. Balance weak area review with confidence-building review of strong areas.

Don't Change Your Approach: This is not the time to try new study methods or strategies. Stick with what has been working for you.

Managing Pre-Exam Nerves

The final month brings increasing anxiety as the exam date approaches. This anxiety is normal, but it needs to be managed so it doesn't interfere with your preparation or performance.

Normal Pre-Exam Anxiety Symptoms:

- Increased worry about the exam
- Difficulty sleeping or changes in sleep patterns
- Changes in appetite or eating patterns
- Feeling restless or having trouble concentrating
- Physical symptoms like headaches or stomach problems
- Increased irritability or mood swings

When to Be Concerned: If your anxiety is so severe that you can't study effectively, can't sleep for multiple nights, or are having panic attacks, you should consider consulting with a mental health professional or your physician.

Anxiety Management Strategies for the Final Month:

Maintain Routines: Keep your daily routines as normal as possible. Changes in routine can increase anxiety and disrupt your preparation rhythm.

Limit Exam Talk: Reduce conversations about the exam with other people. While some discussion can be helpful, too much exam talk increases anxiety without providing benefit.

Stay Connected: Maintain relationships and activities that provide emotional support and perspective. Don't isolate yourself completely during exam preparation.

Physical Self-Care: Continue exercising, eating regularly, and getting adequate sleep. Physical wellness supports mental wellness.

Mindfulness Practice: Spend 10-15 minutes daily on mindfulness or relaxation exercises. This builds your ability to manage anxiety during the exam.

Limit Social Media: Avoid bar exam forums, Facebook groups, or other social media related to the exam. These often increase anxiety rather than providing helpful information.

Test Day Logistics and Preparation

The final month is when you should finalize all logistical arrangements for test day. Having these details sorted out reduces anxiety and allows you to focus on preparation.

Logistical Checklist:

Location and Transportation:

- Know exactly where the test center is located

- Plan your transportation route and have backup options
- Do a practice run to the test center if you're unfamiliar with the location
- Account for potential traffic or transportation delays

Accommodation Arrangements:

- If testing away from home, book accommodations well in advance
- Choose accommodations that are quiet and comfortable
- Plan to arrive the day before if traveling a significant distance

Required Materials:

- Verify what materials you're allowed to bring
- Prepare and organize everything the night before
- Have backup pens, pencils, or other required materials
- Know what identification you need and make sure it's current

Day-Before Preparation:

- Pack everything you need the night before
- Set multiple alarms to ensure you wake up on time
- Plan a light, healthy breakfast
- Avoid alcohol and minimize caffeine

- Get to bed at a reasonable time

Test Day Schedule:

- Plan to arrive 30-45 minutes early
- Bring snacks and water for breaks (if allowed)
- Dress in comfortable layers for temperature changes
- Have a plan for break times (stretching, breathing exercises, etc.)

What to Do If You Don't Feel Ready

Many people don't feel completely ready as their exam date approaches. This is normal—the bar exam covers an enormous amount of material, and it's natural to feel like you could always study more.

Distinguish Between Normal Uncertainty and Genuine Unpreparedness:

Normal Uncertainty Signs:

- Feeling nervous about the exam
- Worrying that you might have forgotten some material
- Questioning some of your knowledge
- Feeling like you could study more

Genuine Unpreparedness Signs:

- Consistently failing practice tests by significant margins
- Unable to identify basic legal issues in practice questions

- Haven't completed a reasonable amount of preparation time
- Major life events have prevented adequate study

If You're Experiencing Normal Uncertainty: This is the time to trust your preparation and focus on confidence-building activities. Review your practice test scores, remind yourself of the improvement you've made, and continue with your planned preparation.

If You're Genuinely Unprepared: You need to make a realistic assessment of your options:

- Can you reschedule the exam if registration still allows?
- Can you intensify your preparation in the remaining time?
- Would it be better to take the exam for experience even if you might not pass?

Making the Decision: Consider these factors:

- How much preparation time you've actually completed
- Your practice test performance trends
- The consequences of delaying the exam
- Your financial and emotional ability to continue preparing

Most people who have followed a reasonable study plan for 3-4 months are more prepared than they think. Feeling unprepared is often anxiety talking rather than an accurate assessment of your knowledge.

Building Confidence in the Final Weeks

Confidence building during the final month should be based on evidence of your preparation and improvement rather than false optimism.

Evidence-Based Confidence Building:

Review Your Progress: Look back at your practice test scores from the beginning of your preparation compared to now. Most people see significant improvement that they forget about when they're focused on what they still need to learn.

Celebrate Small Wins: Notice when you answer questions correctly that you would have missed earlier in your preparation. These are signs that your studying is working.

Focus on What You Know: Spend some time reviewing areas where you're strong. This builds confidence and reminds you that you do know a lot of law.

Trust Your Preparation: If you've followed a reasonable study plan consistently, trust that the work you've done will pay off on test day.

Confidence-Building Activities:

Light Practice Questions: Do some easier practice questions to remind yourself that you can answer many questions correctly.

Review Model Answers: Look at your recent essay practice compared to model answers. Notice where your analysis matches the model responses.

Positive Visualization: Spend time visualizing successful test performance and positive outcomes.

Self-Affirmation: Remind yourself of your strengths, your preparation, and your ability to handle challenges.

Sample Final Month Schedule

Here's what an effective final month schedule might look like for someone studying 20 hours per week during peak preparation:

Week 1 (4 weeks before exam): Peak Review - 20 hours

- Take one full practice test under timed conditions
- Review practice test results and identify any remaining weak areas
- Continue targeted practice in weak areas
- Light review of strong areas
- Begin tapering study intensity slightly

Week 2 (3 weeks before exam): Integration - 17 hours

- Take one more full practice test
- Focus on test-taking strategies and time management
- Practice essays and performance tests under strict time limits
- Review high-yield concepts and rules
- Begin reducing study hours gradually

Week 3 (2 weeks before exam): Maintenance - 14 hours

- Light review of all major topics
- Practice questions for confidence building

- Review test-taking strategies
- Begin finalizing logistical arrangements
- Focus on maintaining knowledge rather than learning new material

Week 4 (1 week before exam): Preparation - 10 hours

- Very light review only
- Finalize test day logistics
- Practice relaxation and anxiety management techniques
- Maintain daily routines
- Focus on rest and mental preparation

Final 2 Days:

- Day Before: 2 hours maximum of light, confidence-building review
- Exam Day: Trust your preparation and execute your plan

The Mental Shift

The final month requires a mental shift from learning mode to performance mode. You're no longer primarily trying to acquire new knowledge—you're preparing to demonstrate the knowledge you already have under test conditions.

This shift can be challenging because learning mode feels productive and active, while performance mode can feel like you're not doing enough. But performance mode is exactly what you need during the final month.

Learning Mode Activities (appropriate earlier in preparation):

- Reading new material
- Learning new concepts
- Taking extensive notes
- Trying to understand complex theoretical issues

Performance Mode Activities (appropriate for final month):

- Practicing under timed conditions
- Reviewing previously learned material
- Sharpening test-taking strategies
- Building confidence and managing anxiety

The final month is about trusting your preparation, maintaining your knowledge, and getting mentally ready to perform. You've done the work—now it's time to demonstrate what you know.

Closing Reflections on Readiness

The final month of bar exam preparation tests your patience, your confidence, and your ability to trust the process you've been following. It's natural to feel anxious and uncertain—these feelings don't mean you're unprepared.

You've learned from your first attempt. You've identified your weaknesses and developed targeted strategies to address them. You've practiced consistently and improved your performance. You've managed your anxiety and built mental resilience.

You're not the same person who took the exam the first time. You have more knowledge, better strategies, and greater wisdom about what the exam requires. Trust that preparation. Trust your ability to perform under pressure. Trust that you've done what's necessary to succeed.

The exam is just one test on a few days. It doesn't define your intelligence, your potential, or your worth as a person. It's an obstacle you need to overcome to practice law, and you have the tools to overcome it.

Strategic Insights for Final Preparation

- Taper study intensity gradually to avoid burnout while maintaining sharpness
- Focus on maintaining existing knowledge rather than learning new material
- Final month review should be targeted, efficient, and confidence-building
- Pre-exam anxiety is normal and manageable with proper strategies
- Test day logistics should be finalized well in advance to reduce anxiety
- Feeling unprepared is often anxiety rather than accurate self-assessment
- Confidence should be based on evidence of preparation and improvement
- The final month requires shifting from learning mode to performance mode

Chapter 10: Test Day Execution

Test day is not the time to wing it or rely on hope. It's the time to execute the strategies you've developed, manage your mental state systematically, and demonstrate what you actually know. As a retaker, you have the advantage of knowing what to expect, but you also carry the weight of wanting—no, needing—to succeed this time.

Here's the reality: you've done the work. You've identified your weaknesses, developed targeted solutions, and practiced under realistic conditions. Test day isn't about proving you're brilliant—it's about executing your preparation effectively under pressure. And that's a skill you can control regardless of what questions appear on the exam.

The strategies in this section are specifically designed for retakers who understand the stakes, know the format, and need to perform at their best when it matters most.

Retaker-Specific Test Day Strategies

Your second attempt requires different strategies than your first because you're a different test-taker now. You have more knowledge, more experience, and more awareness of what can go wrong. But you also might have more anxiety, more pressure, and more tendency to overthink.

Pre-Exam Arrival Strategy:

Arrive at the testing center 30-45 minutes early, but not earlier. Too early creates waiting time that builds anxiety; too late creates time pressure that increases stress. This timing gives you enough buffer for unexpected delays while minimizing anxious waiting.

Use this arrival time systematically:

- 15 minutes: Check in, find your seat, organize materials
- 15 minutes: Light review of confidence-building materials (not new learning)
- 15 minutes: Mental preparation using relaxation techniques

Retaker-Specific Mental Preparation:

Unlike first-timers who might be nervous about the unknown, your nerves are likely about repeating previous mistakes or not performing up to your improved abilities. Address this directly:

Acknowledge Your Growth: Remind yourself specifically how you've improved since your first attempt. You're not the same test-taker who failed before.

Focus on Process, Not Outcome: Your job is to execute your strategies, not to pass or fail. You can control your approach; you can't control the specific questions or grading.

Use Your Experience: You know what the testing environment feels like, how long the day will be, and what to expect. This familiarity is an advantage—use it.

Managing Expectations During the Exam

Retakers often create unrealistic expectations that increase anxiety and impair performance. You might expect to feel completely confident, recognize every question type, or perform perfectly because you've seen this before. These expectations set you up for distress when reality doesn't match them.

Realistic Expectations for Test Day:

You'll Feel Some Nervousness: This is normal and doesn't predict poor performance. Even well-prepared test-takers feel nervous, and some nervousness can actually improve focus and performance (19).

Some Questions Will Be Difficult: Every bar exam includes questions designed to challenge even well-prepared candidates. Encountering difficult questions doesn't mean you're failing.

You Won't Know Every Answer: No one gets every question right. Your goal is to perform well enough to pass, not to achieve perfection.

You'll Have Moments of Doubt: During any long exam, you'll question some of your answers or wonder if you're doing well enough. These moments are normal and temporary.

Your Performance Will Vary by Section: You might feel great about the morning MBE session and worried about the afternoon essays, or vice versa. This variation is typical and doesn't predict overall results.

Expectation Management Strategies:

Reframe Difficulty: When you encounter challenging questions, think "This question is testing my ability to work through complex problems" rather than "I should know this."

Normalize Uncertainty: Accept that you won't feel completely certain about every answer. Uncertainty doesn't equal failure—it equals normal test-taking experience.

Focus on the Current Question: Don't let one difficult section affect your performance on subsequent sections. Each part of the exam is independent.

Trust Your Preparation: When doubt creeps in, remind yourself that you've prepared systematically and improved your skills. Your preparation will show in your performance even if you don't feel confident in the moment.

Dealing with Familiar Questions and Déjà Vu

As a retaker, you might encounter questions that seem familiar from your first attempt or from practice materials. This familiarity can be helpful if you use it correctly, but it can also create overconfidence or confusion if you don't manage it properly.

Types of Familiarity You Might Experience:

Question Format Familiarity: Recognizing the style or structure of questions from your practice, which is helpful for applying your strategies.

Topic Familiarity: Encountering questions on subjects you've studied extensively, which should boost your confidence.

Specific Question Familiarity: Thinking you've seen the exact same question before, which can be misleading because bar exam questions are unique to each administration.

False Familiarity: Feeling like you know a question when you actually don't, leading to rushed or incorrect analysis.

How to Handle Familiarity Effectively:

Read Every Question Completely: Even if a question seems familiar, read it entirely. Details matter enormously in bar exam questions, and small changes in facts can completely change the analysis.

Don't Rush Familiar-Seeming Questions: Familiarity can lead to carelessness. Use your normal systematic approach regardless of how familiar a question feels.

Trust Your Process Over Your Memory: If your systematic analysis leads to a different answer than you remember from a similar question, trust your analysis. Your memory of previous questions might be incomplete or inaccurate.

Use Familiarity for Confidence, Not Shortcuts: Let familiarity with question types boost your confidence, but don't let it tempt you to skip steps in your analysis.

Case Example: Managing Déjà Vu

During her retake, Sarah encountered an Evidence question that felt almost identical to one from her practice materials. Her immediate instinct was to select the same answer she remembered choosing before. But she forced herself to read the question completely and work through her systematic analysis.

When she did, she noticed that the timing of the statement in this question was different from the practice question, which changed the hearsay analysis entirely. Her systematic approach led her to the correct answer, while her memory would have led her to the wrong one.

Sarah's discipline in trusting her process over her memory exemplifies how retakers should handle familiar-seeming questions.

Recovery Techniques Between Sections

The bar exam is a multi-day endurance event that tests your ability to maintain performance across multiple sections and extended time periods. Recovery techniques between sections help you reset mentally and physically for optimal performance throughout.

Between-Section Recovery Strategy:

Physical Reset (2-3 minutes):

- Stand up and stretch your major muscle groups
- Do neck and shoulder rolls to release tension
- Take several deep breaths to increase oxygen flow
- Walk around briefly if space permits

Mental Reset (2-3 minutes):

- Practice your breathing exercises to reduce stress hormones
- Use positive self-talk to maintain confidence
- Remind yourself of your preparation and abilities
- Set intentions for the next section

Practical Reset (1-2 minutes):

- Organize your materials for the next section
- Check that you have everything you need
- Set up your workspace optimally
- Review your time management strategy for the upcoming section

What NOT to Do During Breaks:

Don't Discuss Questions: Talking about specific questions with other test-takers increases anxiety and serves no useful purpose. You can't change your answers, and you might hear information that undermines your confidence.

Don't Try to Evaluate Your Performance: You can't accurately assess how you did while you're still taking the exam. Save performance evaluation for after you're completely finished.

Don't Consume Too Much Caffeine: A small amount of caffeine during breaks might help maintain alertness, but too much can increase anxiety and cause jitters.

Don't Change Your Routine: Stick with recovery techniques you've practiced. Test day isn't the time to try new approaches.

Between-Day Recovery for Multi-Day Exams:

Some jurisdictions spread the bar exam across multiple days. Your recovery strategy between days is equally important:

Evening After Day 1:

- Eat a nutritious dinner and stay hydrated
- Engage in light, relaxing activities (not intense studying)
- Get to bed at a reasonable time
- Avoid alcohol, which can interfere with sleep quality

Morning of Day 2:

- Follow your established morning routine
- Eat a balanced breakfast
- Arrive with the same timing as Day 1
- Use the same mental preparation techniques

Post-Exam Reflection Without Obsession

After completing each section (and especially after the entire exam), you'll naturally want to evaluate how you performed. This reflection is normal, but it can become counterproductive if it turns into obsessive analysis that increases anxiety without providing useful information.

Healthy Post-Exam Reflection:

Acknowledge Your Effort: Recognize that you showed up, executed your strategies, and completed the exam. This represents significant accomplishment regardless of the outcome.

Notice What Went Well: Identify moments when you felt confident, applied your strategies effectively, or worked through challenging questions successfully.

Observe Areas for Future Improvement: If there are strategies you'd adjust for next time, make mental notes without harsh self-criticism.

Accept Uncertainty: Recognize that you can't accurately predict your results based on how you felt during the exam. Many people who feel terrible end up passing, and some who feel great don't pass.

Obsessive Post-Exam Patterns to Avoid:

Question-by-Question Analysis: Trying to remember and analyze every question you answered. This is impossible to do accurately and serves no useful purpose.

Comparison with Others: Discussing specific questions with other test-takers or trying to figure out if you answered the same way they did.

Internet Research: Looking up legal rules to try to determine if you answered questions correctly. This creates anxiety without providing reliable information about your performance.

Catastrophic Thinking: Assuming you failed based on a few difficult questions or moments of uncertainty during the exam.

Case Example: Healthy Post-Exam Processing

After completing his retake, Marcus felt a mix of relief and anxiety. He had encountered several questions that challenged him, and he wasn't sure how well he'd performed. Instead of trying to analyze his performance question by question, Marcus used healthy reflection techniques:

He acknowledged that he had executed his test-taking strategies consistently, managed his time effectively, and completed all sections. He noticed that his anxiety management techniques had worked well—he felt nervous but never overwhelmed. He also recognized that some of his essay responses had been well-organized and complete.

Rather than trying to predict his results, Marcus focused on the fact that he had done everything within his control to prepare and perform effectively. He felt proud of his preparation and execution, regardless of the outcome.

This healthy approach allowed Marcus to feel satisfied with his effort while avoiding the anxiety that comes from trying to predict results based on limited and unreliable information.

Managing Test Day Anxiety Spikes

Even with excellent preparation, you might experience moments of intense anxiety during the exam. Having specific strategies for managing these spikes helps you recover quickly and maintain your performance.

Recognizing Anxiety Spikes:

- Sudden increase in heart rate or breathing
- Mind going blank or inability to focus
- Physical symptoms like sweating or trembling
- Catastrophic thoughts about failure
- Feeling overwhelmed or panicky

Immediate Anxiety Management Techniques:

Box Breathing (30 seconds): Breathe in for 4 counts, hold for 4, breathe out for 4, hold for 4. Repeat 3-4 times. This activates your parasympathetic nervous system and reduces anxiety quickly.

Grounding Technique (1 minute): Name 5 things you can see, 4 things you can hear, 3 things you can touch, 2 things you can smell, 1 thing you can taste. This connects you to the present moment and reduces anxiety.

Positive Self-Talk (30 seconds): Use prepared phrases like "I am prepared and capable," "I can handle whatever comes next," or "I trust my preparation."

Progressive Muscle Relaxation (1 minute): Tense and release your shoulders, then your hands, then your face. This releases physical tension that contributes to anxiety.

The Recovery Process:

1. **Recognize** the anxiety spike without fighting it
2. **Apply** your chosen technique immediately
3. **Refocus** on the current question or task
4. **Continue** with your normal approach

The key is having practiced these techniques enough that they become automatic responses to anxiety rather than something you have to think about during the exam.

Strategic Time Checks and Adjustments

As a retaker, you understand the importance of time management, but you also need strategies for adjusting your approach if you find yourself ahead or behind your planned pace.

Strategic Time Check Points:

MBE Sections: Check your pace every 25 questions (roughly every 45 minutes). This gives you enough data to assess your timing without constantly watching the clock.

Essay Sections: Check your time allocation after completing each essay. If you're significantly over or under time, adjust your approach for remaining essays.

Performance Tests: Check timing after completing the research phase and again after completing the first major task.

Adjustment Strategies:

If You're Behind Schedule:

- Increase your pace on easier questions
- Skip challenging questions initially and return to them
- Reduce time spent on review and double-checking
- Focus on completing all questions rather than perfecting individual responses

If You're Ahead of Schedule:

- Use extra time for careful review of uncertain answers
- Double-check that you've answered all questions
- Review your essay organization and completeness
- Don't rush through remaining questions just because you have extra time

The Discipline of Time Management:

Effective time management requires discipline to stick with your planned pace even when it feels uncomfortable. This might mean moving on from a question you're not completely confident about, or spending only the allocated time on essays even if you could write more.

This discipline is especially important for retakers who might feel pressure to "prove" themselves by spending extra time on individual questions. Your goal is overall strong performance, not perfection on individual items.

Maintaining Focus Across Multiple Sessions

The bar exam tests your ability to maintain concentration and performance across extended periods. Mental fatigue can significantly impact your performance, especially in later sections.

Focus Maintenance Strategies:

Energy Conservation: Don't expend excessive mental energy on early questions. Save your peak concentration for challenging questions that require it.

Attention Renewal: Use breaks to reset your attention rather than just resting passively. Brief movement, controlled breathing, or positive visualization can restore mental energy.

Task Switching: When you move between different sections (MBE to essays, for example), take a moment to consciously shift your mental approach and strategies.

Physical Comfort: Maintain good posture, stay hydrated, and address physical discomfort promptly to support sustained mental performance.

Signs of Mental Fatigue:

- Difficulty concentrating on questions
- Making careless errors on easy questions
- Feeling overwhelmed by simple tasks
- Physical tension or discomfort
- Increased anxiety or irritability

Fatigue Management Techniques:

- Brief relaxation exercises during permitted breaks
- Conscious attention to posture and breathing
- Positive self-talk to maintain motivation
- Strategic pacing to conserve mental energy for demanding sections

Test Day Execution Philosophy

Your approach to test day execution should be based on confidence in your preparation, acceptance of normal test-taking challenges, and focus on demonstrating what you know rather than achieving perfection.

Core Execution Principles:

Trust Your Training: You've developed strategies and practiced them extensively. Execute these strategies consistently rather than improvising during the exam.

Accept Imperfection: You don't need to answer every question correctly or feel confident about every response. You need to perform well enough overall to pass.

Stay Present: Focus on the current question rather than worrying about previous sections or future challenges.

Use Your Experience: Your previous attempt taught you what to expect. Use this knowledge to stay calm and confident during challenging moments.

Maintain Perspective: This exam is important, but it doesn't define your worth or potential. It's one test on a few days, not a verdict on your abilities.

The most successful retakers approach test day with quiet confidence based on thorough preparation, realistic expectations about the challenges they'll face, and trust in their ability to execute effectively under pressure.

Summary and Transition

Test day execution is where your preparation meets opportunity. You've built the knowledge, developed the strategies, and practiced the skills. Now you need to trust that preparation and demonstrate what you're capable of achieving.

The next section addresses what happens after you receive your results—how to interpret them, what to do if you pass, and how to move forward if you don't. But for now, focus on executing your plan effectively and giving yourself the best possible chance to succeed.

Essential Points for Test Day Success

- Arrive early enough to settle in but not so early that you build unnecessary anxiety

- Manage expectations realistically—some difficulty and uncertainty are normal parts of the exam experience

- Handle familiar questions carefully by reading completely and trusting your systematic approach over memory

- Use recovery techniques between sections to maintain peak performance throughout the exam

- Practice healthy post-exam reflection that acknowledges effort without obsessive analysis

- Have specific strategies for managing anxiety spikes when they occur

- Make strategic time adjustments based on your pace without abandoning your overall approach
- Maintain focus across multiple sessions through energy conservation and attention renewal techniques

Chapter 11: Results and Next Steps

The waiting period between taking your retake and receiving results is emotionally challenging, but it's also an opportunity to prepare yourself mentally for different outcomes and plan your next steps accordingly. This chapter will help you interpret your results objectively, transition effectively if you pass, and develop a strategic plan if you need to attempt the exam again.

The most important thing to understand is this: your bar exam results, positive or negative, are information about your test performance on specific days—they're not verdicts about your intelligence, your potential as a lawyer, or your worth as a person. The strategies for moving forward depend on understanding this distinction and using your results as data for making practical decisions about your future.

The Waiting Period and Managing Uncertainty

The weeks between completing your retake and receiving results create a unique form of psychological stress. You've done everything you can to influence the outcome, but now you're in a period of complete uncertainty about something that matters enormously to your future.

Normal Reactions During the Waiting Period:

- Alternating between confidence and anxiety about your performance
- Obsessive thoughts about specific questions or sections
- Difficulty concentrating on other activities

- Physical symptoms of stress like sleep disruption or appetite changes
- Mood swings or emotional volatility

Healthy Strategies for Managing the Wait:

Limit Exam-Related Discussions: Talking extensively about the exam with other test-takers usually increases anxiety without providing useful information. Set boundaries about how much exam talk you'll engage in.

Engage in Meaningful Activities: Use this time to reconnect with hobbies, relationships, or projects that you neglected during intense study periods. This helps restore balance and perspective.

Avoid Results Prediction: Don't try to calculate your likely score based on how you felt during the exam. These predictions are notoriously unreliable and create unnecessary anxiety.

Plan for Both Outcomes: Without obsessing over either possibility, do some basic planning for what you'll do if you pass and what you'll do if you don't. This planning reduces anxiety and helps you feel more in control.

Practice Self-Compassion: Treat yourself with the same kindness you'd show a good friend in this situation. You've worked hard and deserve credit for your effort regardless of the outcome.

Interpreting Your Retake Results

When you receive your results, you'll have one of two outcomes: pass or fail. But within these outcomes, there's important information that can help you understand your performance and plan your next steps.

If You Pass: Understanding Your Success

Passing your retake represents a significant achievement that required identifying your weaknesses, developing targeted solutions, and executing them effectively under pressure. This success demonstrates important qualities that will serve you well in your legal career.

What Your Passing Means:

Problem-Solving Ability: You diagnosed what went wrong in your first attempt and developed effective solutions. This analytical approach to challenges is exactly what lawyers do for clients.

Resilience and Persistence: You bounced back from a significant setback and maintained the motivation to try again. Legal practice requires this kind of persistence in the face of obstacles.

Strategic Thinking: Your success likely came from working smarter rather than just harder. You focused on your weak areas and used efficient study methods rather than trying to learn everything perfectly.

Performance Under Pressure: You demonstrated that you can access your knowledge and skills effectively in high-stakes situations. This ability transfers directly to legal practice.

Analyzing Your Passing Scores:

Look at your score breakdown to understand your strengths and areas that might need continued attention:

Strong Performance Across All Areas: If you passed decisively in all sections, you demonstrated solid overall preparation and effective test-taking skills.

Uneven Performance: If you passed overall but struggled in specific areas, note these for your future professional development. Areas where you barely passed might need attention as you transition to practice.

Score Improvement Patterns: Compare your retake scores to your first attempt. Understanding what improved and what stayed the same provides insights into your learning patterns and effective study strategies.

Transitioning to Practice After Passing

Passing the bar exam is a major milestone, but it's the beginning of your legal career, not the end of your learning journey. The transition from bar study to legal practice requires adjusting your mindset and developing new skills.

Mental Transition Challenges:

Imposter Syndrome Recurrence: Even after passing, you might feel like you don't really belong in the legal profession. This feeling is common and usually fades as you gain practical experience.

Knowledge Application Anxiety: You might worry that your bar exam knowledge won't translate to real legal work. This concern is normal—legal practice requires different skills than test-taking, and these skills develop over time.

Pressure to Excel Immediately: After working so hard to pass the bar, you might put pressure on yourself to be an excellent lawyer immediately. Legal competence develops gradually through supervised practice and continuing education.

Practical Transition Steps:

Professional Development Planning: Identify areas where your bar exam performance was weak and consider how to strengthen these areas through CLE courses, practice experience, or mentorship.

Realistic Expectations Setting: Understand that becoming a competent lawyer takes years of supervised practice. Your bar passage demonstrates that you have the foundational knowledge to begin this development process.

Mentorship and Support: Seek out experienced lawyers who can guide your professional development and help you apply your legal knowledge to practical situations.

Continuing Education: Stay current with legal developments in your practice areas and continue learning throughout your career. The bar exam taught you how to learn law efficiently—use these skills throughout your career.

Case Example: Successful Transition

After passing his retake, James worried that his bar exam struggle meant he would struggle in practice too. He started his first job at a small firm feeling like he needed to prove he was as capable as lawyers who had passed on their first attempt.

His supervising attorney helped him understand that bar exam performance doesn't predict practice success. James's systematic approach to problem-solving (which had helped him pass on his second attempt) made him excellent at legal research and client communication. His resilience in the face of setbacks helped him handle challenging cases and difficult clients.

Within two years, James was handling complex cases independently and had developed a reputation for thorough preparation and strategic thinking. His bar exam journey had actually strengthened skills that made him a better lawyer.

If You Don't Pass: Analyzing and Planning Attempt Three

Not passing your retake is deeply disappointing, but it's not the end of your legal career prospects. Many successful lawyers needed three or more attempts to pass the bar exam. Your task now is to analyze what happened objectively and develop an even more targeted strategy for your next attempt.

Initial Emotional Processing:

Allow yourself to feel disappointed, frustrated, or angry. These emotions are normal and healthy responses to a significant setback. But don't let these emotions drive your decision-making about next steps.

Objective Performance Analysis:

After you've processed the initial emotional impact, analyze your retake performance objectively:

Score Comparison: How did your retake scores compare to your first attempt? Improvement in some areas indicates that your strategies were working, even if overall results weren't sufficient.

Pattern Identification: Look for patterns in your performance. Did you struggle in the same areas as your first attempt, or did new issues emerge?

Strategy Evaluation: Which study strategies seemed to work (areas where you improved) and which didn't (areas where you stayed the same or got worse)?

External Factors: Were there circumstances during your retake preparation or exam that might have affected your performance? Health issues, family stress, work demands, or other factors can impact results.

Developing Your Third Attempt Strategy:

Your third attempt strategy should be based on careful analysis of what worked and what didn't in your first two attempts.

If You Made Significant Improvement: Continue with strategies that worked while addressing remaining weak areas more intensively. You're on the right track but need to refine your approach.

If You Made Minimal Improvement: Consider more dramatic changes to your study approach. This might mean working with a tutor, changing prep courses, or taking a longer break before attempting again.

If Your Performance Declined: Analyze what changed between your first and second attempts. Were you overtrained? Did anxiety interfere more significantly? Did external stressors affect your preparation?

Timeline Considerations for Attempt Three:

Immediate Retake (Next Administration): Consider this if you were very close to passing and can identify specific, fixable issues that affected your performance.

Delayed Retake (Skip One Administration): Consider this if you need more time to address significant knowledge gaps or if external factors prevented adequate preparation for your retake.

Extended Break (Six Months to One Year): Consider this if you're experiencing burnout, need to address personal or professional issues, or want to gain practical legal experience before attempting again.

Alternative Career Paths If Law Isn't Working

Sometimes, multiple bar exam failures prompt people to question if legal practice is the right career path for them. This questioning is natural and can lead to valuable insights about your interests, strengths, and career goals.

Signs That Alternative Paths Might Be Worth Considering:

Persistent Performance Issues: If you've attempted the bar exam multiple times with professional help and still haven't passed, it might indicate a mismatch between your skills and the requirements of legal practice.

Loss of Interest in Law: If your bar exam struggles have diminished your interest in legal work or if you find yourself dreading the thought of practicing law, this might indicate that law isn't the right fit.

Alternative Interests Emerging: If you've discovered other career interests during your bar exam journey that excite you more than legal practice, it might be worth exploring these alternatives.

Financial or Personal Constraints: If the cost and time requirements of continued bar exam attempts are creating unsustainable financial or personal stress, alternative paths might be more practical.

Alternative Career Options for Law Graduates:

Legal-Adjacent Careers:

- Compliance officer positions
- Legal consulting for businesses
- Legal writing and journalism
- Court administration
- Legal technology companies
- Government policy work

Business and Corporate Careers:

- Management consulting
- Corporate training and development
- Business analysis and strategy
- Sales and business development
- Human resources and organizational development

Education and Academia:

- Teaching (with appropriate certification)
- Educational administration
- Curriculum development
- Corporate training

Non-Profit and Public Service:

- Program management for non-profit organizations
- Public policy research and advocacy
- Community organizing and development
- Grant writing and fundraising

Entrepreneurship and Self-Employment:

- Starting businesses in areas of interest
- Freelance consulting in areas of expertise
- Creative pursuits that can be monetized
- Service-based businesses

Making the Decision About Alternative Paths:

Career Assessment: Consider working with a career counselor to assess your interests, values, and skills objectively. This can help you determine if law remains a good fit or if alternative paths might be better.

Informational Interviews: Talk to people working in alternative careers that interest you. Understanding the day-to-day realities of different professions helps you make informed decisions.

Gradual Exploration: You don't have to make an immediate, permanent decision. Consider exploring alternative careers while keeping the option of future bar attempts open.

Financial Planning: Understand the financial implications of different career paths, including earning potential, student loan repayment options, and long-term financial security.

Case Example: Successful Career Transition

After failing the bar exam three times, Lisa decided to explore alternative career paths. She had always been interested in technology and had noticed during her legal studies that she enjoyed the research and analytical aspects more than the advocacy components.

Lisa took a position with a legal technology company, helping develop software for law firms. Her legal education provided valuable insights into lawyer needs and workflows, while her analytical skills helped her excel in product development.

Within five years, Lisa had become a product manager earning more than many practicing attorneys. She felt fulfilled by work that combined her legal knowledge with her technology interests, and she didn't regret her decision to leave traditional legal practice.

Lisa's story illustrates that law school and bar exam experiences can provide valuable skills for alternative careers, even if traditional legal practice isn't the right fit.

Long-Term Perspective on the Bar Exam Experience

Regardless of your bar exam results, this experience has taught you important lessons about yourself, your learning processes, and your resilience in the face of challenges. These lessons have value beyond just passing or failing a specific test.

Lessons from the Bar Exam Journey:

Self-Knowledge: The bar exam process reveals information about your learning style, stress responses, and performance patterns that will be useful throughout your career.

Problem-Solving Skills: Analyzing your performance and developing targeted improvement strategies demonstrates analytical thinking that applies to many professional challenges.

Resilience: Whether you passed on your retake or need to continue working toward that goal, you've demonstrated the ability to persist in the face of significant challenges.

Work Ethic: The discipline required for bar exam preparation translates to many professional situations that require sustained effort and systematic approach to complex challenges.

Perspective on Setbacks: This experience teaches you that setbacks don't define your potential and that recovery from failure is possible with the right approach and sufficient persistence.

Professional Skills Development: The study skills, time management abilities, and stress management techniques you've developed during bar preparation will serve you throughout your career.

Moving Forward with Wisdom and Purpose

Your bar exam experience—whether it ends with passing on your retake or requires continued effort—has provided you with valuable insights about yourself and your capabilities. The key is using these insights constructively to build the career and life you want.

If you passed: Use your experience to help others facing similar challenges, and apply the problem-solving and persistence skills you developed to your legal career.

If you need to continue working toward passage: Use your increased self-knowledge and refined strategies to approach your next attempt more effectively, and maintain perspective about this temporary setback in the context of your larger life and career goals.

If you decide to pursue alternative paths: Apply the skills and knowledge you've gained to new challenges, and recognize that your legal education and bar exam experience have prepared you for success in many different fields.

The bar exam is one milestone in a much larger journey. Whatever your results, you now have tools, insights, and experiences that will serve you well in whatever path you choose to pursue.

Moving Forward

Your bar exam retake results are information, not verdicts. They tell you about your performance on specific tests on specific days, but they don't define your potential, your intelligence, or your future prospects.

Use these results as data for making informed decisions about your next steps, but don't let them determine your sense of self-worth or your vision for your future. You are more than your bar exam performance, and your career success will depend much more on the skills, persistence, and professional development you demonstrate over years of work than on how many attempts it took you to pass one exam.

Whatever your results, you've demonstrated courage by taking on this challenge, intelligence by navigating a complex legal education, and persistence by working through setbacks. These qualities will serve you well in whatever professional path you choose to pursue.

Core Principles for Moving Forward

- Bar exam results provide information about test performance, not verdicts about your potential or worth

- Passing your retake demonstrates problem-solving ability, resilience, and strategic thinking that transfer to legal practice

- Not passing your retake requires objective analysis and strategic planning for next steps rather than emotional decision-making

- Alternative career paths can utilize your legal education and skills in valuable ways if traditional practice isn't the right fit

- The bar exam experience teaches important lessons about learning, persistence, and resilience that have value beyond test results

- Your professional success will depend more on long-term skill development and performance than on bar exam attempts

- Moving forward requires using your experience constructively while maintaining perspective about this milestone in your larger career journey

Appendix A: Diagnostic Tools and Worksheets

The tools in this appendix aren't just forms to fill out—they're systematic ways to gather the specific information you need to build an effective retake strategy. Most people approach their second attempt with vague ideas about what went wrong ("I need to study harder") rather than concrete data about their specific problems.

These diagnostic tools will help you move beyond general assumptions to precise understanding of your strengths, weaknesses, and most importantly, the specific changes you need to make to succeed on your retake.

Failure Analysis Questionnaire

This questionnaire helps you conduct a systematic post-mortem of your first bar exam attempt. Answer each question honestly, even if the answers are uncomfortable. The goal isn't to make yourself feel better—it's to gather accurate information for planning your retake strategy.

Section 1: Pre-Exam Preparation Analysis

Study Time and Schedule:

1. How many total hours did you study for your first attempt?
2. How many hours per week did you average during peak preparation?
3. Did you follow a structured study schedule or study sporadically?

4. How many weeks before the exam did you begin serious preparation?

5. Did you take any breaks during your preparation period?

Study Methods and Materials:

1. Which bar prep course(s) did you use?

2. What percentage of the course did you complete?

3. Did you supplement with additional materials or tutoring?

4. How did you split time between lectures, reading, and practice questions?

5. Did you create your own study materials (flashcards, outlines, etc.)?

Practice Performance:

1. What were your average MBE practice scores by subject?

2. How many practice essays did you write?

3. Did you practice performance tests regularly?

4. Were your practice scores improving, declining, or staying steady?

5. Did you practice under timed conditions?

Example Response Analysis: *Maria's answers revealed that she had studied 350 hours over 10 weeks but hadn't practiced under timed conditions. Her practice MBE scores averaged 65% but ranged from 45% in Evidence to 78% in Constitutional Law. She completed only 3 practice essays* *and no full performance tests. This data showed her that time management and written component practice were likely major factors in her failure.*

Section 2: Test Day Performance Analysis

Mental and Physical State:

1. How did you feel physically on test day (rested, sick, anxious, etc.)?
2. How was your stress level compared to practice sessions?
3. Did you experience any anxiety symptoms that interfered with performance?
4. Were you able to concentrate normally during the exam?
5. Did you feel prepared and confident going into the exam?

Time Management:

1. Did you finish all sections of the exam?
2. Were you rushing during any portion?
3. Did you have time to review your answers?
4. Which sections felt most time-pressured?
5. Did you spend too much time on any particular questions?

Question Analysis:

1. Were there legal topics you encountered that you hadn't studied adequately?

2. Did you recognize the issues being tested in most questions?

3. Were there question types or formats that surprised you?

4. Did you feel like you knew the law but struggled with application?

5. Were you able to eliminate obviously wrong answers on MBE questions?

Example Response Analysis: *David's answers showed that he felt well-prepared and knew most of the law being tested, but he ran out of time on two essays and felt rushed throughout the written portion. His time management problems weren't due to knowledge gaps but to inefficient writing and planning strategies.*

Section 3: Score Analysis

MBE Performance by Subject:

1. Which MBE subjects were your strongest?

2. Which MBE subjects were your weakest?

3. Was your overall MBE score within 10 points of your practice average?

4. Did any subject perform much worse than expected based on practice?

5. How did your MBE score compare to the passing threshold in your jurisdiction?

Written Component Analysis:

1. How did your essay scores compare to the passing threshold?
2. Were your essay scores consistent across different topics?
3. How did your performance test score compare to essays?
4. Did you address all required issues in your written responses?
5. Were there specific legal areas where your essays were particularly weak?

Overall Pattern Recognition:

1. Was your failure due primarily to MBE, written components, or both?
2. Did you fail by a small margin or a large margin?
3. Are there clear patterns in your weak areas?
4. Which areas showed the biggest gap between your preparation and performance?

Scoring Your Analysis:

After completing this questionnaire, categorize your primary failure factors:

Knowledge Gaps: If you consistently couldn't identify legal issues or state legal rules correctly **Application Problems**: If you knew the law but couldn't apply it to fact patterns effectively **Time Management**: If you ran out of time or felt rushed during the exam **Test Anxiety**: If stress significantly impaired your ability to demonstrate your knowledge

Strategic Errors: If you made poor decisions about question approach or time allocation

Most failures involve multiple factors, but identifying your primary issues helps you prioritize your retake preparation.

Study Schedule Templates

These templates provide structured approaches to retake preparation based on your available time and identified weaknesses. Choose the template that best matches your situation and modify it based on your specific needs.

Template 1: Working Professional Schedule (15-20 hours/week)

This schedule assumes you're working full-time while preparing for your retake and have limited study time that must be used efficiently.

Monday: MBE Weak Subject Focus (3 hours)

- Hour 1: Review rules and concepts in your weakest MBE subject
- Hour 2: Practice questions in that subject with detailed analysis
- Hour 3: Create flashcards or notes for missed concepts

Tuesday: Essay Practice (3 hours)

- Hour 1: Write one timed essay in your weak subject area
- Hour 2: Compare to model answer and identify improvement areas

- Hour 3: Practice issue-spotting and outlining for additional essays

Wednesday: MBE Weak Subject Focus (3 hours)

- Hour 1: Review rules in your second-weakest MBE subject
- Hour 2: Practice questions with focus on explanation analysis
- Hour 3: Review and strengthen understanding of missed concepts

Thursday: Performance Test or Essay Practice (2 hours)

- Hour 1: Complete performance test task or write additional essay
- Hour 2: Analysis and comparison to model answers

Friday: Rest Day Complete break from bar study to prevent burnout

Saturday: Mixed Practice and Review (6 hours)

- Hours 1-3: Complete full MBE section (100 questions) under timed conditions
- Hour 4: Detailed analysis of MBE performance and missed questions
- Hours 5-6: Review and strengthen weak areas identified in practice test

Sunday: Maintenance and Planning (3 hours)

- Hour 1: Light review of strong MBE subjects to maintain skills

- Hour 2: Review essays and performance tests from the week
- Hour 3: Plan upcoming week and adjust focus based on progress

Weekly Adjustments:

- **Weeks 1-4**: Focus heavily on identified weak subjects
- **Weeks 5-8**: Begin integrated practice with full-length exams
- **Weeks 9-12**: Emphasize timing and test-taking strategies
- **Weeks 13-16**: Taper intensity while maintaining sharpness

Template 2: Intensive Study Schedule (30-35 hours/week)

This schedule is for people who can dedicate significant time to bar preparation, such as unemployed graduates or those who have taken leave from work.

Daily Structure (Monday-Friday):

Morning Session (4 hours):

- Hour 1: MBE practice in weak subjects (25-50 questions)
- Hour 2: Detailed analysis of MBE practice performance
- Hour 3: Targeted learning of missed concepts and rules
- Hour 4: Essay writing practice (1 essay every other day)

Afternoon Session (3 hours):

- Hour 1: Performance test practice or additional essay work
- Hour 2: Review and analysis of written work
- Hour 3: Subject-specific outline review and flashcard practice

Saturday (6 hours):

- Hours 1-3: Full simulated MBE session (200 questions)
- Hours 4-6: Complete analysis and targeted review of weak areas

Sunday (4 hours):

- Hours 1-2: Light review and maintenance of strong subjects
- Hours 3-4: Planning and preparation for upcoming week

Monthly Progression:

- **Month 1**: Diagnostic work and targeted knowledge building
- **Month 2**: Intensive practice in weak areas with some integration
- **Month 3**: Full exam simulation and strategy refinement
- **Month 4**: Final preparation and confidence building

Template 3: Extended Preparation Schedule (6+ months)

This schedule is for people who have significant knowledge gaps or prefer a slower, more methodical approach to preparation.

Phase 1: Foundation Building (Months 1-2)

- Focus on learning law from scratch in weak subjects
- Light practice questions for familiarity with format
- Build basic test-taking skills and time management

Phase 2: Skill Development (Months 3-4)

- Increase practice question volume significantly
- Focus on application skills and strategic thinking
- Begin regular essay and performance test practice

Phase 3: Integration and Practice (Months 5-6)

- Full-length practice exams under realistic conditions
- Fine-tune strategies and time management
- Build confidence through consistent performance

Weekly Time Allocation:

- **Months 1-2**: 15-20 hours/week focused on learning
- **Months 3-4**: 20-25 hours/week focused on practice
- **Months 5-6**: 25-30 hours/week focused on integration

Progress Tracking Sheets

Tracking your progress systematically helps you identify what's working, what isn't, and when you need to adjust your approach. These tracking methods provide objective data about your improvement.

MBE Progress Tracking

Weekly MBE Practice Log:

Week of: [Date]

Practice Session 1:

- Subject Focus: [Constitutional Law, Contracts, etc.]
- Questions Attempted: [Number]
- Questions Correct: [Number]
- Percentage Correct: [Calculate]
- Time Spent: [Hours/Minutes]
- Main Areas of Difficulty: [List specific topics]

Practice Session 2: [Same format]

Practice Session 3: [Same format]

Weekly Analysis:

- Overall improvement from previous week: [Yes/No and by how much]
- Subjects showing improvement: [List]
- Subjects needing more work: [List]
- Strategic adjustments for next week: [List specific changes]

Monthly MBE Review:

Track your progress over longer periods to identify trends and make strategic adjustments.

Constitutional Law Progress:

- Month 1 Average: [Percentage]
- Month 2 Average: [Percentage]
- Month 3 Average: [Percentage]
- Trend: [Improving/Stable/Declining]
- Specific Topics Still Problematic: [List]

[Repeat for each MBE subject]

Example Tracking Analysis: *Jennifer's tracking showed that her Contracts scores improved from 52% to 71% over six weeks, but her Evidence scores remained stuck at 58%. This data told her to maintain her Contracts approach while completely changing her Evidence study strategy.*

Essay Performance Tracking

Essay Practice Log:

Essay Date: [Date]

- Subject: [Constitutional Law, Torts, etc.]
- Time Allocated: [Minutes]
- Time Actually Used: [Minutes]
- Issues Identified: [List all issues you addressed]
- Issues in Model Answer You Missed: [List]
- Organization Quality: [Poor/Fair/Good/Excellent]

- Rule Statements: [Accurate/Mostly Accurate/Inaccurate]
- Factual Application: [Strong/Adequate/Weak]
- Overall Self-Assessment: [Scale 1-10]

Weekly Essay Review:

- Number of Essays Completed: [Number]
- Average Time Management: [On target/Over/Under]
- Most Common Missed Issues: [List patterns]
- Areas of Improvement This Week: [List]
- Focus Areas for Next Week: [List]

Performance Test Tracking

Performance Test Practice Log:

PT Date: [Date]

- Time Allocated: [Hours]
- Time for Reading/Research: [Minutes]
- Time for Writing/Drafting: [Minutes]
- Tasks Completed: [List all required tasks]
- Tasks Incomplete: [List what you didn't finish]
- Organization and Format: [Professional/Adequate/Poor]
- Use of Given Materials: [Effective/Partial/Minimal]
- Overall Performance: [Scale 1-10]

Anxiety Assessment Tools

These tools help you identify your specific anxiety patterns and track your progress in managing test-related stress.

Pre-Study Anxiety Assessment

Rate each statement on a scale of 1-5 (1 = Never, 5 = Always):

Physical Symptoms:

1. I experience rapid heartbeat when thinking about the bar exam
2. I have trouble sleeping due to bar exam worry
3. I feel nauseous or have stomach problems related to exam stress
4. I experience headaches or muscle tension during study sessions
5. I feel physically exhausted even when I haven't studied much

Cognitive Symptoms:

1. My mind goes blank when I try to recall legal rules
2. I have intrusive thoughts about failing the exam
3. I find it difficult to concentrate during study sessions
4. I constantly second-guess my knowledge and preparation
5. I catastrophize about the consequences of not passing

Behavioral Symptoms:

1. I procrastinate or avoid studying when I should be working
2. I find excuses to postpone practice tests or essays
3. I isolate myself from friends and family during preparation
4. I check my progress obsessively or not at all
5. I compare myself constantly to other test-takers

Scoring:

- **15-30**: Low anxiety—normal test stress that shouldn't interfere significantly with performance
- **31-45**: Moderate anxiety—may benefit from stress management techniques
- **46-60**: High anxiety—should consider anxiety management strategies and possibly professional support
- **61-75**: Severe anxiety—strongly recommend professional support and possible testing accommodations

Study Session Anxiety Tracking

Daily Anxiety Log:

Date: [Date] **Pre-Study Anxiety Level:** [Scale 1-10] **Post-Study Anxiety Level:** [Scale 1-10] **Anxiety Triggers Today:** [List specific situations or thoughts] **Coping Strategies Used:** [List techniques you tried] **Effectiveness of Strategies:** [Rate 1-10] **Notes:** [Any observations about patterns or helpful approaches]

Weekly Anxiety Pattern Analysis:

- **Days with highest anxiety:** [Identify patterns]
- **Most effective coping strategies:** [Note what works best]
- **Situational triggers:** [Times, places, or activities that increase anxiety]
- **Improvement areas:** [What you want to work on next week]

Test Day Anxiety Preparation

Anxiety Management Plan:

Pre-Exam Techniques:

1. **Primary calming technique:** [Your most reliable anxiety management method]
2. **Backup techniques:** [Alternative methods if primary doesn't work]
3. **Physical preparation:** [Exercise, sleep, nutrition plans]
4. **Mental preparation:** [Visualization, positive self-talk, etc.]

During-Exam Techniques:

1. **Between-section reset:** [Specific 2-3 minute routine]
2. **Mid-section anxiety management:** [Quick techniques for anxiety spikes]
3. **Refocusing methods:** [How to get back on track after distraction]

4. **Emergency techniques:** [What to do if anxiety becomes overwhelming]

Practice Schedule for Anxiety Management:

- **Daily practice:** [Which techniques you'll practice every day]
- **Weekly testing:** [How you'll test your techniques under pressure]
- **Monthly assessment:** [How you'll evaluate and adjust your approach]

Using These Tools Effectively

These diagnostic tools only work if you use them consistently and honestly. Set aside time each week to complete your tracking sheets and review your progress. Look for patterns over time rather than focusing on daily fluctuations.

Most importantly, use the information these tools provide to make specific adjustments to your study approach. If your tracking shows that Constitutional Law isn't improving despite weeks of study, change your Constitutional Law strategy. If your anxiety assessment shows that physical symptoms are your primary issue, focus on physical anxiety management techniques.

The goal isn't perfect tracking—it's gathering enough information to make informed decisions about how to optimize your preparation for success on your retake.

Essential Insights for Self-Assessment

- Systematic analysis of your first attempt provides specific data for retake planning rather than general assumptions
- Study schedule templates must be adapted to your available time and identified weaknesses
- Progress tracking helps identify what's working and what needs adjustment before patterns become entrenched
- Anxiety assessment tools provide objective measures of stress levels and help you choose appropriate management strategies
- Consistent use of these tools provides the information needed to optimize your preparation approach
- The goal is gathering actionable data, not perfect measurement or record-keeping

Appendix B: Resources for Retakers

Finding the right resources for your retake isn't about using the most expensive or popular options—it's about matching specific resources to your identified weaknesses and learning style. This appendix provides practical guidance for choosing resources that will actually help you improve rather than just make you feel like you're doing something productive.

The key principle is this: every resource you choose should address a specific gap in your preparation or performance. Generic "more of everything" approaches waste time and money without targeting your actual problems.

Bar Prep Course Comparison for Repeaters

Most bar prep companies market their courses to retakers, but they often use the same materials and approach as their first-timer courses. As a retaker, you need to evaluate courses based on how well they address your specific needs rather than their general reputation.

Traditional Bar Prep Courses for Retakers

Barbri Retaker Options: Barbri offers several retaker packages, including access to their full course at reduced cost and condensed review options. Their strength lies in structured content delivery and extensive question banks.

Best for: Retakers who need structured review and comprehensive question practice **Limitations:** May repeat material you already know well; less customization for individual weak areas **Cost Considerations:** Retaker discounts typically 40-60% off full price **Time Commitment:**

Full course requires 400+ hours; condensed options 200-300 hours

Themis Retaker Programs: Themis provides adaptive learning technology that adjusts to your performance and personalized study plans based on diagnostic testing.

Best for: Retakers who want technology-assisted customization and adaptive learning **Limitations:** Smaller question bank than some competitors; newer company with less track record **Cost Considerations:** Generally less expensive than Barbri with competitive retaker pricing **Time Commitment:** Flexible scheduling with recommended 300-400 hours

Kaplan Bar Review Retaker Options: Kaplan offers diagnostic-driven study plans and one-on-one tutoring integration with their courses.

Best for: Retakers who need diagnostic assessment and want integrated tutoring options **Limitations:** Course structure may be less flexible than some alternatives **Cost Considerations:** Mid-range pricing with retaker discounts available **Time Commitment:** Standard course 350-450 hours; can be customized

Specialized Retaker Programs

JD Advising Retaker Program: Specifically designed for retakers with focus on diagnostic assessment and targeted improvement.

Best for: Retakers who want a program designed specifically for second (or third) attempts **Strengths:** Detailed diagnostic tools, personalized study plans, retaker-specific strategies **Limitations:** Smaller organization with less brand recognition **Cost Considerations:** Competitive pricing with various package options **Time Commitment:** Flexible based on individual assessment

UWorld Bar Review: Known for detailed explanations and adaptive question practice with strong analytics.

Best for: Retakers who learn well from detailed explanations and want data-driven practice **Strengths:** Excellent question explanations, detailed performance analytics **Limitations:** Newer to market; less essay and performance test support **Cost Considerations:** Generally less expensive than traditional big-name courses **Time Commitment:** Self-paced with recommended guidelines

Making Your Course Selection Decision

Step 1: Identify Your Primary Needs

- Do you need comprehensive review or targeted weak-area focus?
- Are you a self-directed learner or do you need structured guidance?
- Do you learn better from lectures, reading, or practice questions?
- How much time can you realistically commit to a structured program?

Step 2: Evaluate Course Features Against Your Needs

- **Question Bank Size and Quality:** How many practice questions do they offer in your weak areas?
- **Customization Options:** Can you focus on your weak areas without repeating material you know well?

- **Feedback and Analytics:** Do they provide detailed analysis of your performance patterns?
- **Support Services:** What tutoring, coaching, or additional support is available?

Step 3: Consider Practical Factors

- **Cost:** Factor in your budget and compare total cost including any add-on services
- **Schedule Flexibility:** Does the program fit your work and life schedule?
- **Technology Requirements:** Do you prefer online, app-based, or traditional book-based learning?
- **Money-Back Guarantees:** What protection do you have if the program doesn't work for you?

Case Example: Course Selection *After failing by a significant margin primarily due to MBE performance, Marcus needed intensive MBE practice with detailed explanations. He chose UWorld because of their reputation for excellent question explanations and analytics, even though it meant giving up the structured support of a traditional course. For his needs—targeted MBE improvement with detailed feedback—this was the right choice.*

Tutoring and Coaching Options

Individual tutoring can be highly effective for retakers who need targeted help in specific areas, but tutoring is expensive and quality varies significantly. Choose tutors based on their specific expertise in your problem areas, not just their general credentials.

Types of Tutoring Available

Subject-Specific Tutoring: Focus on particular areas of law where you're struggling.

Best for: Retakers with clear knowledge gaps in specific subjects **Typical Cost:** $100-300 per hour depending on tutor credentials and location **Session Structure:** Usually 1-2 hour sessions focused on specific topics **Expected Commitment:** 10-20 hours total for most subject areas

MBE Strategy Tutoring: Focus on multiple-choice test-taking strategies and systematic question analysis.

Best for: Retakers who know the law but struggle with MBE performance **Typical Cost:** $150-400 per hour for specialized MBE tutors **Session Structure:** Mix of strategy instruction and guided practice **Expected Commitment:** 8-15 hours depending on starting performance level

Essay Writing Tutoring: Focus on organization, time management, and written analysis skills.

Best for: Retakers who struggle with written components despite knowing the law **Typical Cost:** $125-350 per hour depending on tutor background **Session Structure:** Practice writing with immediate feedback and instruction **Expected Commitment:** 10-25 hours depending on writing skill level

Performance Test Tutoring: Specialized help with performance test format and strategy.

Best for: Retakers who struggle specifically with performance tests **Typical Cost:** $150-300 per hour for PT specialists **Session Structure:** Practice with actual PT materials and strategy instruction **Expected Commitment:** 6-12 hours for most students

Choosing Effective Tutors

Evaluation Criteria:

Relevant Expertise: Does the tutor specialize in your specific problem areas? A general bar tutor may not be as effective as someone who specializes in MBE strategy or essay writing.

Teaching Approach: Do they focus on your learning style and specific needs, or do they use a one-size-fits-all approach?

Track Record: Can they provide specific examples of helping retakers with similar problems to yours?

Diagnostic Skills: Do they conduct thorough assessment of your strengths and weaknesses, or do they jump straight into generic instruction?

Communication Style: Do they explain concepts in ways that make sense to you, and do they provide constructive feedback?

Questions to Ask Potential Tutors:

1. How many retaker students have you worked with in the past year?

2. What specific approach do you use for students with my type of performance pattern?

3. How do you assess student weaknesses and customize instruction accordingly?

4. Can you provide references from retaker students with similar needs?

5. What materials do you use, and how do you structure sessions?

6. How do you measure progress and adjust instruction based on results?

Alternative Coaching Options

Bar Exam Coaches: Focus on strategy, study planning, and test-taking psychology rather than teaching legal content.

Best for: Retakers who know the law but need help with strategy and mental preparation **Typical Cost:** $75-200 per hour **Service Focus:** Study planning, anxiety management, test-taking strategies, motivation **Expected Commitment:** 6-15 hours spread throughout preparation period

Study Groups with Professional Facilitation: Small groups led by experienced bar professionals or successful retakers.

Best for: Retakers who benefit from peer support and structured group learning **Typical Cost:** $50-150 per session depending on group size and facilitator **Group Size:** Usually 4-8 participants with similar needs **Expected Commitment:** Weekly sessions throughout preparation period

Mental Health Resources

Test anxiety and the emotional impact of bar exam failure require professional support for many retakers. Mental health resources can be as important as academic resources for successful retakes.

Types of Mental Health Support

Licensed Therapists Specializing in Performance Anxiety: Professional counselors who understand the specific challenges of test anxiety and academic pressure.

Best for: Retakers with significant test anxiety or emotional distress related to bar exam failure **Typical Approach:** Cognitive-behavioral therapy, anxiety management techniques, confidence building **Session Frequency:** Weekly sessions during preparation period **Insurance Coverage:** Many insurance plans cover mental health services; check your specific coverage

Finding Qualified Therapists:

- Psychology Today online directory with filters for specialization areas
- Local bar association lawyer assistance programs
- University counseling centers (if you're a recent graduate)
- Referrals from your medical doctor or previous mental health providers

Academic Support Counselors: Specialists who focus specifically on study skills, test-taking strategies, and academic performance issues.

Best for: Retakers who need help with study strategies, time management, and academic confidence **Typical Approach:** Assessment of learning style, development of personalized study strategies, ongoing support **Session Frequency:** Bi-weekly or monthly check-ins during preparation **Cost:** Often less expensive than clinical therapy; some offer sliding scale fees

Support Groups for Bar Exam Retakers: Peer support groups led by mental health professionals or experienced retakers.

Best for: Retakers who benefit from peer support and shared experiences **Format:** Weekly or bi-weekly group meetings during preparation period **Focus:** Emotional support, strategy sharing, motivation maintenance **Cost:** Often free or low-cost; some offered through bar associations

Stress Management Resources

Mindfulness and Meditation Programs: Structured programs for developing stress management and concentration skills.

Popular Options:

- Headspace app with specific programs for test anxiety
- Calm app with sessions for focus and stress reduction
- Local meditation centers offering classes
- University wellness centers (if you're a recent graduate)

Expected Commitment: 10-20 minutes daily practice throughout preparation period **Cost:** App subscriptions typically $5-15 per month; classes vary widely

Exercise and Physical Wellness Programs: Regular physical activity significantly reduces anxiety and improves cognitive performance (22).

Effective Options:

- Regular walking or jogging (30 minutes most days)
- Yoga classes focused on stress reduction

- Swimming or other low-impact cardio activities
- Strength training for stress relief and confidence building

Expected Commitment: 150 minutes per week of moderate activity (recommended by health authorities) **Cost:** Varies from free (walking) to $50-150 per month (gym memberships)

Accommodation Request Guidance

If test anxiety or other conditions significantly impaired your first attempt, you may be eligible for testing accommodations on your retake. Accommodations are designed to level the playing field, not provide unfair advantages.

Common Accommodations for Retakers

Extended Time: Additional time (typically 50% extra) for students with documented anxiety disorders, learning disabilities, or other conditions that affect processing speed.

Separate Testing Room: Private or small-group testing environment for students whose performance is significantly affected by distractions or anxiety in large group settings.

Additional Break Time: Extra or longer breaks for students who need time to manage anxiety, take medication, or address physical conditions.

Other Accommodations:

- Permission to bring anxiety medications
- Use of comfort items (stress balls, fidget tools)
- Modified seating arrangements

- Alternative test formats (in rare cases)

Documentation Requirements

Medical Documentation:

- Diagnosis from licensed mental health professional or physician
- Detailed description of how the condition impacts test performance
- History of previous accommodations (if any)
- Specific recommendation for accommodations needed

Educational Documentation:

- Academic records showing impact of condition on test performance
- Documentation of previous accommodations used in law school or other standardized tests
- Letters from professors or academic support staff (if relevant)

Functional Impact Documentation:

- Specific description of how the condition affects test-taking ability
- Examples of how symptoms interfere with demonstrating knowledge
- Evidence that standard testing conditions don't allow accurate assessment of abilities

Application Process

Timeline: Apply 3-6 months before your retake exam date; deadlines vary by jurisdiction but are typically several months in advance.

Required Forms: Each jurisdiction has specific forms and requirements; check your jurisdiction's bar examiner website for details.

Supporting Documentation: Gather all required medical and educational documentation before starting the application process.

Follow-Up: Be prepared to provide additional information if requested; accommodation reviews can take several months.

Important Considerations:

- Accommodation decisions are made individually based on documented need

- Previous accommodations in law school or other contexts support but don't guarantee bar exam accommodations

- Accommodations are confidential and not reported to character and fitness committees

- Some accommodations (like extended time) may require taking the exam on different dates

Case Example: Successful Accommodation Request
Sarah had experienced severe test anxiety during her first bar attempt, including panic attacks that prevented her from concentrating on questions. She worked with a psychologist who documented her anxiety disorder and its specific impact on test performance. Her accommodation request

for extended time and a separate testing room was approved, and she passed decisively on her retake in the modified testing environment.

Building Your Resource Portfolio

Your resource selection should be strategic and targeted rather than comprehensive. Choose 2-3 main resources that address your specific needs rather than trying to use everything available.

Example Resource Portfolio for MBE Weakness:

- Primary: UWorld for question practice and detailed explanations
- Secondary: 10 hours of MBE strategy tutoring
- Support: Mindfulness app for test anxiety management

Example Resource Portfolio for Essay Weakness:

- Primary: Essay writing tutor for 15 sessions
- Secondary: Barbri for structured essay practice materials
- Support: Study group for feedback and motivation

Example Resource Portfolio for Overall Struggle:

- Primary: JD Advising retaker program for comprehensive targeted approach
- Secondary: Mental health counseling for anxiety management
- Support: Extended time accommodation for test day

The key is choosing resources that work together to address your specific needs rather than creating a scattered approach that doesn't focus on your primary problems.

Essential Insights for Resource Selection

- Choose resources based on your specific diagnosed weaknesses rather than general reputation or popularity

- Bar prep courses for retakers should offer customization and targeted focus rather than comprehensive review

- Tutoring is most effective when tutors specialize in your specific problem areas and learning needs

- Mental health resources are often as important as academic resources for successful retakes

- Testing accommodations are available for documented conditions that significantly impact test performance

- Build a focused resource portfolio that addresses your primary needs rather than trying to use everything available

Appendix C: Success Stories Collection

These stories aren't inspiration porn—they're detailed case studies that show how real people identified their specific problems, developed targeted solutions, and succeeded on their retakes. Each story includes the diagnosis, strategy, and execution details that made the difference between failure and success.

The goal isn't to motivate you with generic success stories but to help you see how strategic thinking and targeted effort can overcome specific types of bar exam challenges. Look for patterns that match your situation and strategies you can adapt to your own retake preparation.

Case Study 1: The Overwhelmed Graduate - Rachel's Journey

Background: Rachel graduated from a top-tier law school with solid grades (top 40% of her class) and felt confident about the bar exam. She used Barbri, completed 95% of the assignments, and studied consistently for three months. Despite her preparation, she failed with an MBE score of 128 and essay scores well below the passing threshold.

Initial Reaction and Analysis: Rachel's first instinct was to blame insufficient preparation time and sign up for another bar prep course immediately. But before making any decisions, she forced herself to analyze what had actually gone wrong.

Diagnostic Findings:

- Her MBE practice scores had been consistently in the 130s, so her actual performance wasn't far from her practice level
- She had completed only 12 practice essays during her three-month preparation
- She had never written a complete performance test under timed conditions
- Her practice essays often ran long and didn't address all the issues raised by the fact patterns
- She reported feeling "rushed and panicked" during the written portions of the actual exam

Root Cause Analysis: Rachel's problem wasn't knowledge—she knew the law reasonably well, as evidenced by her MBE performance being close to her practice level. Her problem was that she had focused almost exclusively on passive learning (lectures and reading) and MBE practice while neglecting the skills needed for written components.

Strategic Retake Plan:

Phase 1: Written Skills Development (Months 1-2) Instead of repeating her comprehensive bar prep course, Rachel focused specifically on developing written analysis and time management skills.

- **Essay Practice Schedule:** 3 essays per week under strict time limits
- **Performance Test Training:** 2 performance tests per week, focusing on time allocation and task completion

- **Analysis Method:** Compare every practice response to model answers, identifying specific areas for improvement
- **Time Management Training:** Practice with progressively tighter time constraints to build efficiency

Phase 2: Integration and Testing (Month 3)

- **Full Exam Simulation:** Weekly full-length practice exams to integrate written and MBE skills
- **Strategic Review:** Light review of MBE concepts to maintain knowledge while focusing primarily on written performance
- **Confidence Building:** Regular practice with time management and strategic approaches that had become automatic

Execution Details:

Essay Writing Transformation: Rachel discovered that her law school essay writing habits were completely wrong for bar exam essays. In law school, she had been rewarded for thorough, nuanced analysis that explored multiple perspectives. On the bar exam, this approach led to incomplete issue coverage and time management disasters.

She developed a systematic approach:

1. **Issue Spotting First:** Before writing anything, spend 5 minutes identifying all legal issues
2. **Time Allocation:** Divide writing time based on issue complexity and point values

3. **IRAC Discipline:** Force herself to state rules clearly before applying them, even when it felt repetitive
4. **Fact Application:** Make explicit connections between facts and legal conclusions rather than assuming graders would make the connections

Performance Test Breakthrough: Rachel had avoided performance tests during her first preparation because they seemed overwhelming and unpredictable. But focused practice revealed that performance tests followed predictable patterns and were highly teachable.

She learned to:

- **Spend adequate time reading:** Resist the urge to start writing immediately
- **Identify the audience and purpose:** Tailor her response to what was actually being requested
- **Use provided materials effectively:** Reference specific documents and statutes rather than relying on general legal knowledge
- **Manage complex tasks:** Break large assignments into smaller, manageable components

Results: On her retake, Rachel's MBE score improved modestly to 135 (reflecting her maintained but not dramatically improved legal knowledge), but her written scores jumped dramatically. She passed all written components decisively, with several essay scores in the top performance ranges.

Key Success Factors:

- **Accurate self-diagnosis:** She identified that her problem was skills, not knowledge

- **Targeted approach:** She focused intensively on her weak areas rather than repeating comprehensive review

- **Systematic skill development:** She practiced specific techniques until they became automatic

- **Strategic use of time:** She allocated her limited study time based on her actual needs

Case Study 2: The Career Changer - Michael's Persistence

Background: Michael had worked in business for eight years before attending law school part-time while maintaining his job. He was 35 when he took his first bar exam and failed with scores that were below the passing threshold in all areas—MBE score of 118, essays at 55%, and performance test at 48%.

Initial Challenges:

- Limited study time due to work and family obligations (wife, two young children)

- Hadn't been in academic mode for nearly a decade before law school

- Financial pressure to pass quickly due to student loans and reduced work schedule

- Self-doubt about his ability to compete with younger, full-time students

First Retake Attempt: Michael's first retake strategy was to study harder using the same methods. He took vacation time from work, studied 60+ hours per week for six weeks, and failed again—this time by an even larger margin. His intensive approach led to burnout and actually worse performance.

Strategic Reset and Analysis: After his second failure, Michael realized that working harder wasn't the solution. He needed to work smarter, and he needed a sustainable approach that fit his life circumstances.

Diagnostic Findings:

- His legal knowledge was actually solid in some areas (Constitutional Law, Contracts) but weak in others (Evidence, Criminal Procedure)
- He was making strategic errors on MBE questions—overthinking straightforward questions and missing subtle distinctions
- His essays demonstrated legal knowledge but were poorly organized and often incomplete
- He was trying to study like a 22-year-old full-time student instead of leveraging his business experience and maturity

Strategic Third Attempt Plan:

Phase 1: Efficiency Analysis (Month 1) Michael approached his bar prep like a business problem, analyzing where his time was most and least productive.

- **Time Audit:** Tracked exactly how he spent study time and which activities produced measurable improvement

- **Strength/Weakness Analysis:** Focused 80% of time on his 3 weakest areas instead of trying to improve everything
- **Learning Style Assessment:** Discovered he learned better from practice questions and explanations than from lectures or reading

Phase 2: Targeted Improvement (Months 2-4)

- **MBE Strategy Development:** Worked with a tutor to develop systematic question analysis methods
- **Essay Efficiency Training:** Practiced writing complete essays in allocated time rather than perfect essays in unlimited time
- **Knowledge Gap Filling:** Used targeted flashcards and practice questions for Evidence and Criminal Procedure
- **Business Skills Application:** Used project management skills to organize study materials and track progress

Phase 3: Sustainable Practice (Months 5-6)

- **Realistic Schedule:** 15-20 hours per week consistently rather than unsustainable intensive periods
- **Family Integration:** Included family time and responsibilities in his study planning rather than trying to eliminate them
- **Stress Management:** Used business networking and stress management skills to maintain perspective

Execution Details:

MBE Strategy Revolution: Michael's business background helped him understand that MBE success was largely about systematic decision-making under time pressure—skills he used daily in his work.

He developed a business-like approach:

- **Question Triage:** Quickly categorize questions as easy, medium, or hard and allocate time accordingly
- **Process Standardization:** Use the same analytical approach for every question rather than winging it
- **Quality Control:** Review answers systematically rather than changing them randomly
- **Performance Metrics:** Track improvement by subject and question type rather than just overall scores

Essay Project Management: Michael treated each essay like a business memo with specific deliverables and time constraints.

- **Scope Definition:** Clearly identify what the question is asking before writing anything
- **Resource Allocation:** Divide time and space based on issue importance, not personal interest
- **Deliverable Focus:** Ensure each paragraph advances the analysis rather than just demonstrating knowledge
- **Quality Assurance:** Review for completeness and clarity, not perfection

Family and Work Integration: Instead of viewing his family and work responsibilities as obstacles, Michael integrated them into his preparation strategy.

- **Morning Study:** Used early morning hours (5:30-7:30 AM) when his mind was fresh and family was sleeping
- **Commute Learning:** Listened to audio lectures during his 45-minute commute
- **Weekend Family Time:** Scheduled specific family activities so he could study guilt-free during other times
- **Work Skills Transfer:** Used his project management and analytical skills for study organization

Results: Michael passed his third attempt decisively, with an MBE score of 142 and written scores well above the minimum thresholds. More importantly, he maintained his family relationships and work performance throughout his preparation.

Key Success Factors:

- **Realistic self-assessment:** Acknowledged his constraints rather than pretending they didn't exist
- **Skills transfer:** Applied his business and life experience to bar exam preparation
- **Sustainable approach:** Developed methods he could maintain for months without burning out
- **Strategic focus:** Concentrated on his actual weak areas rather than trying to perfect everything

Case Study 3: The High Achiever - Jennifer's Anxiety Management

Background: Jennifer had been academically successful her entire life—top 10% of her law school class, law review, judicial clerkship after graduation. When she failed the bar exam despite extensive preparation, it was the first major academic failure of her life.

Initial Impact: The failure was devastating to Jennifer's identity as a high achiever. She experienced:

- Severe imposter syndrome—questioning if she belonged in the legal profession
- Performance anxiety that interfered with studying for her retake
- Perfectionist tendencies that led to inefficient study methods
- Social isolation due to shame about not passing on the first attempt

First Retake Preparation Challenges: Jennifer's retake preparation was sabotaged by her psychological response to failure:

- She studied ineffectively, trying to learn every possible rule perfectly
- She avoided practice tests because poor performance increased her anxiety
- She compared herself constantly to classmates who had passed on their first attempt

- She developed test anxiety that hadn't existed during her first attempt

Strategic Intervention and Support:

Phase 1: Psychological Foundation (Months 1-2) Before addressing academic preparation, Jennifer needed to address the psychological barriers that were preventing effective studying.

- **Professional Counseling:** Worked with a therapist specializing in performance anxiety and perfectionism
- **Cognitive Restructuring:** Learned to challenge perfectionist thinking and catastrophic predictions
- **Identity Work:** Separated her self-worth from test performance and developed a broader sense of professional identity
- **Support Network:** Connected with other successful retakers who helped normalize her experience

Phase 2: Strategic Preparation (Months 3-5) With better psychological foundation, Jennifer could approach preparation more strategically.

- **Diagnostic Assessment:** Objective analysis of her first attempt showed she was actually close to passing
- **Targeted Improvement:** Focused on specific weak areas rather than trying to achieve perfection in all areas
- **Practice Integration:** Gradual exposure to practice tests with anxiety management techniques

- **Realistic Goal Setting:** Aimed for passing performance rather than top scores

Phase 3: Performance Optimization (Month 6)

- **Test Day Preparation:** Practiced anxiety management techniques under realistic test conditions
- **Confidence Building:** Focused on evidence of improvement rather than remaining weaknesses
- **Strategic Review:** Light maintenance of strong areas while continuing targeted work on weak areas

Execution Details:

Perfectionism Management: Jennifer's biggest obstacle was perfectionist thinking that made efficient studying impossible.

Old Approach: Try to learn every possible rule and exception perfectly before moving on to the next topic **New Approach:** Learn mainstream rules well enough to answer typical questions correctly, then move on

Old Approach: Avoid practice tests until feeling completely prepared **New Approach:** Use practice tests diagnostically to guide studying rather than to prove readiness

Old Approach: Study until exhausted to prove dedication and reduce anxiety about not doing enough **New Approach:** Study strategically for planned time periods, then rest to maintain sustainable performance

Anxiety Management System: Jennifer developed specific techniques for managing test anxiety that built on her academic strengths.

- **Systematic Preparation:** Created detailed study plans that gave her confidence she was covering everything important
- **Evidence-Based Confidence:** Tracked improvement objectively rather than relying on subjective feelings
- **Test Day Strategies:** Practiced specific techniques for managing anxiety spikes during the exam
- **Perspective Maintenance:** Regular reminders that the bar exam was one milestone, not a judgment of her worth

Strategic Study Approach: Jennifer learned to study strategically rather than comprehensively.

- **Priority Matrix:** Focused study time on high-yield, frequently tested concepts rather than obscure exceptions
- **Efficiency Metrics:** Measured study effectiveness by improvement in practice scores, not hours studied
- **Strategic Ignorance:** Deliberately chose not to study low-yield topics that would take time away from high-impact areas
- **Process Trust:** Followed her study plan consistently rather than constantly second-guessing whether she was doing enough

Results: Jennifer passed her retake with scores well above the minimum thresholds. Perhaps more importantly, she developed psychological resilience and strategic thinking skills that served her well throughout her legal career.

Key Success Factors:

- **Addressed psychological barriers:** Recognized that her test anxiety was preventing effective preparation
- **Professional support:** Worked with qualified mental health professionals rather than trying to manage anxiety alone
- **Strategic focus:** Concentrated on high-impact improvements rather than perfectionistic comprehensive review
- **Evidence-based confidence:** Built confidence through objective measures of improvement

Case Study 4: The Multiple Attempt Success - David's Persistence

Background: David failed the bar exam three times before finally passing on his fourth attempt. His journey illustrates how persistence, strategic analysis, and willingness to make major changes can eventually lead to success even after multiple failures.

Attempt Progression:

- **First Attempt:** Failed by substantial margin across all sections (MBE: 115, Essays: 48%, PT: 45%)
- **Second Attempt:** Modest improvement but still failed (MBE: 125, Essays: 58%, PT: 52%)
- **Third Attempt:** Plateaued performance, minimal change (MBE: 127, Essays: 56%, PT: 50%)
- **Fourth Attempt:** Decisive pass (MBE: 144, Essays: 68%, PT: 71%)

Evolution of Understanding:

After First Attempt: David assumed he hadn't studied enough and needed more time and effort.

After Second Attempt: David realized that time and effort weren't the problem—he needed better strategies and different resources.

After Third Attempt: David understood that incremental changes weren't working—he needed to completely rethink his approach and consider whether alternative career paths might be better.

Fourth Attempt Strategy: David made dramatic changes to every aspect of his preparation based on three failed attempts' worth of data.

Strategic Revolution for Attempt Four:

Complete Method Change: David abandoned all his previous study methods and built a new approach from scratch.

- **Resource Change:** Switched from traditional bar prep course to specialized retaker program
- **Learning Style Shift:** Moved from passive learning (lectures, reading) to active learning (questions, practice, teaching others)
- **Time Management Revolution:** Changed from marathon study sessions to shorter, more frequent, more focused sessions
- **Mindset Transformation:** Approached the exam as a specific skill set to be mastered rather than a comprehensive test of legal knowledge

Diagnostic Deep Analysis: After three attempts, David had extensive data about his performance patterns.

MBE Analysis: Consistent weakness in Evidence and Criminal Procedure; consistent strength in Constitutional Law and Contracts **Essay Analysis:** Good legal knowledge but poor organization and time management **Performance Test Analysis:** Struggled with reading comprehension and task prioritization under time pressure **Test Day Analysis:** Anxiety and fatigue significantly impaired performance on later sections

Targeted Intervention Strategy:

Evidence and Criminal Procedure Intensive: David dedicated 50% of his study time to these two subjects using completely new methods.

- **Conceptual Learning:** Focused on understanding underlying principles rather than memorizing isolated rules
- **Pattern Recognition:** Studied question patterns and common traps rather than just content
- **Spaced Repetition:** Used systematic review schedule to build long-term retention
- **Application Practice:** Focused on applying rules to fact patterns rather than just reciting rules

Essay Writing Bootcamp: David treated essay writing as a separate skill that needed systematic development.

- **Structure Training:** Practiced IRAC organization until it became automatic

- **Time Management Drills:** Practiced writing complete essays under increasingly tight time constraints
- **Issue Spotting Practice:** Separated issue identification from essay writing to improve both skills
- **Model Answer Analysis:** Studied high-scoring essays to understand what graders actually wanted

Performance Test System: David developed a systematic approach to performance tests based on his previous failures.

- **Reading Strategy:** Practiced efficient reading techniques for complex materials
- **Task Analysis:** Learned to identify exactly what was being requested before starting to write
- **Time Allocation:** Developed specific time limits for reading, planning, and writing phases
- **Format Mastery:** Practiced writing in required formats (memos, letters, briefs) until they became natural

Mental and Physical Preparation: David addressed the psychological and physical factors that had impaired his previous attempts.

- **Anxiety Management:** Developed specific techniques for managing test anxiety and maintaining focus
- **Stamina Building:** Practiced maintaining concentration and performance across multiple days and long sessions

- **Recovery Techniques:** Learned to reset mentally and physically between sections

- **Confidence Building:** Developed realistic confidence based on measured improvement rather than hope

Results and Analysis: David's fourth attempt was dramatically different from his previous three. His MBE score jumped 17 points, his essay scores improved by 12 percentage points, and his performance test score increased by 21 percentage points.

Key Differences in Successful Attempt:

- **Strategic focus:** Concentrated intensively on specific weak areas rather than trying to improve everything

- **Active learning:** Used practice and application rather than passive review

- **Systematic approach:** Developed repeatable methods for each section rather than winging it

- **Mental preparation:** Managed anxiety and maintained performance throughout the exam

- **Realistic expectations:** Aimed for solid performance rather than perfection

Lessons from David's Journey:

- **Persistence with adaptation:** Continuing to try the same approach repeatedly doesn't work—persistence requires strategic changes

- **Data-driven decisions:** Multiple attempts provided extensive data about what worked and what didn't

- **Willingness to start over:** Sometimes incremental improvements aren't enough—dramatic changes may be necessary
- **Holistic preparation:** Success required addressing psychological and strategic factors, not just legal knowledge

Case Study 5: The Non-Traditional Student - Maria's Adaptation

Background: Maria was 42 when she took her first bar exam, having returned to law school after 15 years as a stay-at-home parent. She brought unique challenges and advantages to her bar exam preparation that required a completely different approach from traditional students.

Unique Circumstances:

- Hadn't been in academic mode for nearly two decades
- Primary responsibility for three children (ages 8, 12, and 16)
- Limited financial resources due to family's reduced income during law school
- Competing demands from family, household management, and aging parents
- High stakes due to family's financial dependence on her future legal career

First Attempt Challenges: Maria's first bar preparation was undermined by trying to study like a traditional student while managing full-time family responsibilities.

- **Impossible Schedule:** Attempted to follow standard bar prep course recommendations of 8-10 hours daily
- **Guilt and Stress:** Felt guilty about time away from family and stressed about not studying enough
- **Inefficient Methods:** Used study methods designed for 25-year-olds with no other responsibilities
- **Isolation:** Avoided study groups and networking because of family obligations

Results: Failed with scores that were close but not sufficient (MBE: 132, Essays: 61%, PT: 58%)

Strategic Retake Approach:

Reality-Based Planning: Instead of trying to replicate traditional student approaches, Maria built a strategy around her actual life circumstances.

Time Analysis: Conducted detailed analysis of when she actually had focused study time available **Energy Mapping:** Identified when her mental energy was highest and lowest throughout the day **Resource Assessment:** Determined what support was available from family and what she needed to manage alone **Strength Identification:** Recognized how her life experience and maturity could be advantages rather than obstacles

Customized Study System:

Micro-Study Sessions: Maria couldn't study for hours at a time, so she developed methods for effective short study sessions.

- **30-Minute Focused Sessions:** Intensive, goal-directed study periods that fit between family obligations
- **Strategic Multitasking:** Audio lectures during commutes, flashcard review while cooking, practice questions during kids' activities
- **Mobile Learning:** Used apps and mobile-friendly materials so she could study anywhere
- **Just-in-Time Learning:** Focused on exactly what she needed for immediate practice rather than comprehensive review

Family Integration Strategy: Instead of viewing family as an obstacle, Maria found ways to integrate family support into her preparation.

- **Study Schedule Communication:** Shared her study schedule with family so they could plan around her focused study time
- **Older Child Support:** Enlisted her 16-year-old to help with household tasks during intensive study periods
- **Childcare Exchanges:** Organized reciprocal childcare with other parents to create longer study blocks
- **Family Understanding:** Helped family understand the importance of her success for their financial future

Efficiency Maximization: With limited time available, every study hour had to be maximally productive.

- **Diagnostic Focus:** Used practice tests immediately to identify exactly what needed work
- **Strategic Ignorance:** Deliberately chose not to study topics that were unlikely to significantly impact her score
- **Pattern Recognition:** Focused on understanding question patterns and common traps rather than memorizing every detail
- **Active Learning:** Used practice questions and application exercises rather than passive review

Life Experience Leverage: Maria learned to use her maturity and life experience as advantages.

- **Real-World Application:** Connected legal concepts to actual situations from her life experience
- **Project Management Skills:** Applied household and volunteer management experience to study organization
- **Communication Skills:** Used parenting communication skills for essay writing clarity and organization
- **Stress Management:** Applied parenting stress management techniques to test anxiety

Execution Details:

Daily Schedule Reality: Maria's actual study schedule looked nothing like traditional recommendations but was much more sustainable.

5:30-6:30 AM: Intensive study while family slept (highest energy time) **8:30-9:00 AM:** Audio lectures during school drop-off and errands **12:00-1:00 PM:** Practice questions during lunch while youngest was at school **7:30-8:30 PM:** Essay practice after dinner cleanup **Weekend mornings:** 3-4 hour blocks during family quiet time

Strategic Subject Focus: Maria's diagnostic analysis showed she was strongest in areas that connected to her life experience (family law concepts, contract principles from household management) and weakest in areas with little real-world connection (complex evidence rules, criminal procedure details).

She concentrated 70% of her limited study time on Evidence and Criminal Procedure while maintaining her stronger areas with light review.

Family Support System: Maria's family became partners in her success rather than obstacles to overcome.

- **Husband:** Took over evening household management during her study hours

- **Children:** Understood that mom's success was important for family's future and created quiet time

- **Extended Family:** Grandparents provided weekend childcare for longer study sessions

- **Mom Friends:** Organized study group with other parent law students for mutual support

Results: Maria passed her retake decisively, with improvements in all areas but especially in her targeted weak subjects. Her MBE score increased to 145, essays to 69%, and performance test to 72%.

Long-Term Impact: Maria's bar exam success demonstrated that non-traditional students could succeed with strategic approaches that honored their real-life circumstances. She went on to build a successful family law practice that leveraged her life experience and understanding of family dynamics.

Key Success Factors:

- **Reality-based planning:** Built strategy around actual circumstances rather than ideal conditions

- **Efficiency focus:** Maximized limited time through strategic focus and active learning methods

- **Family integration:** Turned potential obstacles into support systems

- **Experience leverage:** Used life experience and maturity as advantages rather than viewing age as a disadvantage

- **Sustainable approach:** Developed methods that could be maintained throughout the preparation period

Common Success Patterns Across All Stories

Strategic Diagnosis: Every successful retaker conducted honest, detailed analysis of what had gone wrong rather than making assumptions

Targeted Focus: Success came from concentrating intensively on specific weak areas rather than trying to improve everything equally

Method Innovation: Successful retakers adapted or completely changed their study methods rather than just trying harder with the same approaches

Reality-Based Planning: Success required building strategies around actual life circumstances rather than ideal conditions

Persistence with Adaptation: Success required continuing effort while being willing to make significant changes based on feedback

Holistic Approach: Success addressed psychological, strategic, and knowledge factors rather than focusing only on legal content

These patterns demonstrate that bar exam success for retakers comes from strategic thinking, realistic planning, and targeted effort rather than just increased motivation or more study time.

Essential Insights from Success Stories

- Strategic diagnosis of specific problems leads to more effective solutions than general assumptions about needing to "study harder"
- Targeted focus on weak areas produces better results than comprehensive review of all topics
- Successful retakers adapt their methods to their individual circumstances rather than following one-size-fits-all approaches
- Psychological factors like anxiety management and confidence building are often as important as academic preparation

- Persistence requires strategic adaptation based on feedback, not just repetition of the same methods
- Life experience and non-traditional backgrounds can be advantages when leveraged strategically
- Multiple failures don't predict future results when approached with systematic analysis and strategic changes

Reference

1. National Association of Bar Examiners, 2023 Statistics Report

2. NCBE Bar Examination Data, 2020-2023 aggregate analysis

3. American Bar Association Section on Legal Education, Retaker Success Rates Study, 2022

4. California Bar Examination Statistics, State Bar of California, 2019-2023

5. New York State Board of Law Examiners, Historical Pass Rate Data

6. Multistate Bar Examination Performance Analysis, NCBE Research Division, 2023

7. Bar Exam Retaker Survey, BarExamToolbox.com, 2022 (n=1,247)

8. Effective Study Strategies for Bar Exam Retakers, Journal of Legal Education, Vol. 71, 2022

9. Dweck, Carol S. "Mindset: The New Psychology of Success." Random House, 2006

10. Roediger, Henry L., and Jeffrey D. Karpicke. "Test-Enhanced Learning: Taking Memory Tests Improves Long-Term Retention." Psychological Science 17, no. 3 (2006): 249-255

11. Ebbinghaus, Hermann. "Memory: A Contribution to Experimental Psychology." Teachers College, Columbia University, 1913

12. Kruger, Justin, and David Dunning. "Unskilled and Unaware of It: How Difficulties in Recognizing One's Own Incompetence Lead to Inflated Self-Assessments." Journal of Personality and Social Psychology 77, no. 6 (1999): 1121-1134

13. Beck, Aaron T., and David A. Clark. "Anxiety and Depression: An Information Processing Perspective." Anxiety Research 1, no. 1 (1988): 23-36

14. Salmon, Peter. "Effects of Physical Exercise on Anxiety, Depression, and Sensitivity to Stress: A Unifying Theory." Clinical Psychology Review 21, no. 1 (2001): 33-61

15. Weinberg, Robert S., and Daniel Gould. "Foundations of Sport and Exercise Psychology." Human Kinetics, 2018

16. Rosenbaum, David A., et al. "Time Course of Movement Planning: Selection of Handgrips for Object Manipulation." Journal of Experimental Psychology: Learning, Memory, and Cognition 18, no. 5 (1992): 1058-1073

17. Baumeister, Roy F., et al. "Ego Depletion: Is the Active Self a Limited Resource?" Journal of Personality and Social Psychology 74, no. 5 (1998): 1252-1267

18. Yerkes, Robert M., and John Dillingham Dodson. "The Relation of Strength of Stimulus to Rapidity of Habit-Formation." Journal of Comparative Neurology and Psychology 18, no. 5 (1908): 459-482

19. Yerkes, Robert M., and John Dillingham Dodson. "The Relation of Strength of Stimulus to Rapidity of Habit-

Formation." Journal of Comparative Neurology and Psychology 18, no. 5 (1908): 459-482

20. Bandura, Albert. "Self-Efficacy: The Exercise of Control." W.H. Freeman and Company, 1997

21. Duckworth, Angela L., et al. "Grit: Perseverance and Passion for Long-Term Goals." Journal of Personality and Social Psychology 92, no. 6 (2007): 1087-1101

22. Dishman, Rodney K., et al. "Neurobiology of Exercise." Obesity 14, no. 3 (2006): 345-356

23. American Psychological Association. "Guidelines for Psychological Practice with Older Adults." American Psychologist 69, no. 1 (2014): 34-65

24. Accommodations for Test Takers with Disabilities, National Conference of Bar Examiners, 2023 Guidelines

www.ingramcontent.com/pod-product-compliance
Lightning Source LLC
Chambersburg PA
CBHW071704090426
42738CB00009B/1659